Horizons

Spelling and Vocabulary

3

Teacher's Guide

Author:
Rachelle Wiersma, M.A.

Managing Editor:
Alan Christopherson, M.S.

Editor:
Laura Messner, B.A.

Graphic Design & Illustration:
Ron A. Hartmann, B.A.

Alpha Omega Publications, Inc. • Rock Rapids, IA

©MMX by Alpha Omega Publications, Inc.® All rights reserved.

804 N. 2nd Ave. E., Rock Rapids, IA 51246-1759

No part of this publication may be reproduced, stored in an electronic retrieval system, or transmitted in any form by any means—electronic, mechanical, photocopy, recording or otherwise—without the prior written permission of Alpha Omega Publications, Inc. Brief quotations may be used in literary review. All trademarks and/or service marks referenced in this material are the property of their respective owners. Alpha Omega Publications, Inc. makes no claim of ownership to any trademarks and/or service marks other than their own and their affiliates', and makes no claim of affiliation to any companies whose trademarks may be listed in this material, other than their own.

Printed in the United States of America

ISBN 978-0-7403-1957-0

Spelling and Vocabulary 3

Contents

Introduction

Introduction

"Whatever you do, work at it with all your heart, as working for the Lord, not for men."
(Colossians 3:23)

Approaches to Spelling have changed over the years from simple rote memorization of words, often outside any context, to an integrated study of words in relation to their use in the language. Spelling programs, today, move in many directions. Most present some selection of words to be studied, memorized, and used in a written context. Others present guidelines for approaching spelling, but leave the choice of words to the teacher who must then determine which words the students need to know how to spell for successful completion of writing assignments and the study of individual subjects. Whichever approach is taken, most programs agree that words must be studied within the context of the language and that words must be used in a written context.

Horizons Spelling Program Features

The program presents word lists chosen from lists of most frequently used words, sight words, and words chosen for particular phonetic or rhyming patterns. Each lesson also supplies space for four additional "challenge words"—words chosen by the teacher or parent that apply to the student's experience. These "challenge words" can be taken from other subject areas or chosen on an individual basis from words frequently used, but misspelled, in the student's daily writing.

The program is divided into 160 lessons that can be covered in a 32-week period of time, by completing 5 lessons per week. Each week's lessons include 15 spelling words and 5 challenge words. Four review units are spread through the year at Weeks 8, 16, 24, and 32. This division should accommodate classroom schedules for the school year. Home schooling schedules, which are more flexible, may choose to take more or less time depending on the student's progress.

A Spelling dictionary is provided for the spelling words. This dictionary is presented as a separate volume from the Spelling text so that the students may use it more easily and avoid having to move back and forth from the lesson to the back of the book. Space is also provided at the end of the dictionary for the additional "challenge words" selected for each week. Students enter their words in the dictionary each week, writing them under the appropriate letter of the alphabet.

The *Spelling Dictionary* and this *Teacher's Guide* also contain a cumulative word list from *Horizons Spelling Grades 1-3*.

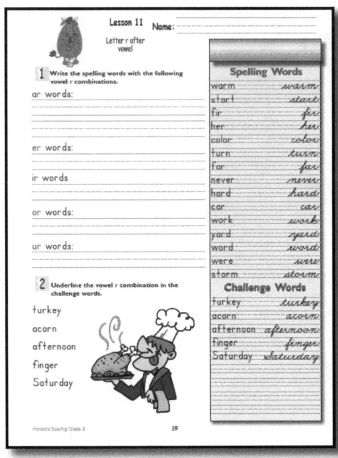

Weekly Schedule

The approach used to teach words for the week is:

Day 1: Assess student's knowledge and introduce words

Day 2: Examine and explore words

Day 3: Look at context and meaning of words

Day 4: Apply understanding of words in writing

Day 5: Assess and evaluate progress

The *Horizons Spelling Program* provides pages for assessment within the context of the week's lessons. The first page of each new set of lessons is entitled "What Do You Know?" The last page of each set is for testing, correction, and practice.

What Do You Know?

This page is a simple assessment tool to see what students already know about the spelling words for the week. It is NOT used as a PRE-TEST. No grades are kept.

The words for the week are said aloud by the teacher, repeated in the context of a sentence, then repeated again.

1. The students write each word as they think it is spelled on the numbered guidelines.

2. When all words have been given, the teacher then looks at the words and writes the corrections for misspelled words next to those that are incorrect. This process is extremely important for the following reasons:

   • It gives the teacher an insight into the student's understanding of words and sounds.

   • It gives the teacher an early indication of problems, such as reversals of letters.

   • It also gives the teacher an opportunity to work with the student, complimenting all efforts and correctly spelled words (or even parts of words), encouraging the student, and helping the student approach the spelling of unknown words.

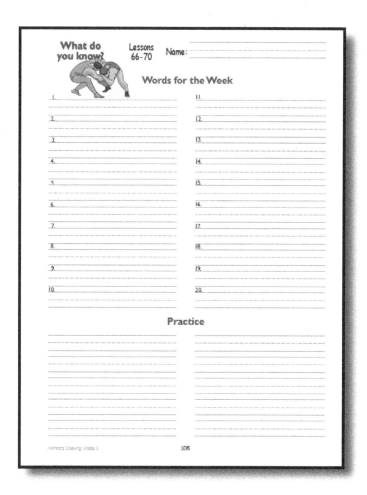

3. The students then practice writing the corrected words in the Practice section.

4. The second side of the page provides the student's first "official" look at the words for the week. Go over the words one by one. Introduce the listed words and the challenge words provided or chosen for the week.

5. Help the students to write two sentences using some of the words for the week. This may be done initially as a class project in which one sentence is written on the board for the entire class to copy, but it should move to the point where students can write their own sentences. The *Spelling Dictionary* provides a sample sentence for each spelling word.

6. Practice space is given for all the spelling words including the challenge words for the week.

This second page may be used as extra in-class work or sent home as a study guide.

Check-Up Time!

The final page of each week's work (Lessons 5, 10, 15, 20, 25, etc.) is an assessment page. Teachers/parents of home schoolers can decide what will be assessed. If a child did exceptionally well on the "What do you know?" pre-assessment, the teacher may choose not to test words already known by the child. The teacher may also choose to test all words for the week. Space is provided for the word list given, but make sure that the four challenge words for the week are tested. It may be wise to keep a notebook on each child in which you will record words that present particular difficulties. These words could be added to review lists or used to replace words already mastered in a review unit.

1. The teacher says the word, repeats it in the context of a sentence, then repeats the word.

Words for the Week

small ball call because walk sauce straw chalk naughty paws tall
water wash talk law basketball macaw Utah laundry faucet

1 Write two sentences using your spelling words.

2 Practice your spelling words. Don't forget your challenge words.

66

Horizons Spelling Grade 3

Check-up time! Lesson 90 Name:

Spelling Test

1.	13.
2.	14.
3.	15.
4.	16.
5.	17.
6.	18.
7.	19.
8.	20.
9.	21.
10.	22.
11.	23.
12.	24.

Corrections

Horizons Spelling Grade 3 143

2. The child writes the word dictated in the Spelling Test section.

3. The process is repeated until all words have been tested.

4. The teacher may correct in class by writing the words on the board.

5. The teacher then uses the correction space provided to write any corrections for words misspelled.

6. On the second side of the Lesson, the student practices the correct spelling of any words missed.

7. By folding over the practice part of the page, a section is provided for retesting or for testing additional sight or "challenge words" added for the week.

Rules

Spelling/phonics rules that apply to the lessons are included in the teacher's guide rather than in the student book. They are listed at the beginning of each week's lessons. The rules can be copied to poster board for bulletin board use. Students can make individual "rule books" by copying the rules to sheets of paper that are placed in a binder or notebook. Go over the rules with the students at the beginning of each week's lesson and throughout the week as they are applied to the words being practiced.

Penmanship

Both manuscript and cursive examples are given for the weekly Spelling Words and Challenge Words. These examples are consistent with the penmanship styles taught in other products of the Horizons curriculum. These styles can be followed or the style being learned by the student from other materials. Where possible, guidelines have been provided to promote good penmanship. Any penmanship requirements are left up to the teacher.

To promote good penmanship the lesson pages should be removed from the workbook at the perforation. This gives the student a flat page on which to write.

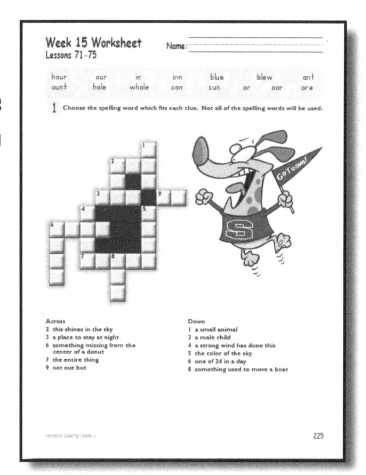

Reproducible Worksheets

A worksheet for each week is included as a reproducible master. It may be used in class or as a homework assignment. The worksheet answer keys appear on the page that begins each week's information in the Teacher's Guide.

Answer Keys

Reduced student pages are included with the instructional information that is provided in the Teacher's Guide for each lesson. The answers for the student activities appear on the reduced student pages. Sample sentences are also included for the open-ended sentence writing activities. These can be used to help the students develop their own sentences for the words in the activity.

Materials for Extended Practice and Activities

1. Classroom charts of word families can be made and posted to help the students see the relationships between words.

2. Have a spelling notebook for each student. In this notebook, they will have two sections: (1) they will write sentences for all of their spelling words each week; (2) they will write definitions for all of their "choice" challenge words for the week. These two weekly activities may be done in class or as homework. Since each lesson has 24 words, have the students divide their sentence writing over several days; i.e., 6 or 7 sentences per day for 4 days. When the activities in the Spelling book include writing sentences, the number in the notebook is reduced. The definitions of "choice" words should be done early in the week. Check the notebooks weekly, commenting on the good points and providing additional practice for those words and English skills that need reinforcement. Word processing programs, blogs, and other electronic options could also be used for all or parts of the notebook.

3. A Language Arts or Spelling Learning Center can be created in the room. Materials can include:

   - At least two sets of flash cards of the spelling words for the week: one set of complete words, one set in which the words are divided into syllables.

   - A set of flash cards can be made of the spelling rules. The flashcards for the spelling words can then be grouped into the rule category that applies to the word.

   - Word family pages for the week's words with blank pages to add new words.

   - A scrabble-type game to encourage spelling of new words.

   - Story starters for each week's lessons. These can be made using pictures from magazines or other sources. Look for pictures that include some of the spelling words for the week. Mount the pictures on cards and keep in a folder. Have lined paper available so that the students can go to the center, choose a picture, and write about it. Pictures are then returned to the folders when the student finishes the story.

   - A set of alphabet cards and a cumulative set of spelling word cards to be used for practicing dividing words into the correct ABC order.

Spelling Dictionary

The *Spelling Dictionary* is an integral part of the Horizons Spelling Program and accomplishes several purposes:

1. Students will become acquainted with the format and function of a simple dictionary.

2. Students will learn the function of guide words and diacritical markings.

3. Students will be able to see and read their spelling words within the context of a sentence.

4. Students will be able to identify basic parts of speech.

5. Students will have an opportunity to practice their alphabetizing and reading/writing skills by using the *Spelling Dictionary* to perform the following tasks:

   - Look up the spelling words at the beginning of each week's lessons.

   - Record their weekly assigned "Challenge Words" in the appropriate location at the back of the *Spelling Dictionary*.

   - Use the *Spelling Dictionary* as a resource for writing sentences and stories.

Word Lists

Included with this guide are two different word lists. The Horizons Spelling 3 Word List contains the words taught and practiced each week in this grade level. The Horizons Spelling Grades 1-3 Cumulative Word List includes an alphabetic listing of all the words covered in Grades 1-3 of the Horizons Spelling program.

The Grade 3 weekly lists can be used in several ways:

1. The teacher can use them as a quick reference for what is coming next.

2. The teacher can use them as a master list for assessment each week.

3. Weekly word lists can be duplicated for the students to take home for practice.

4. There is a week of review each nine weeks in this course and cumulative lists can be duplicated to send home for additional study and practice.

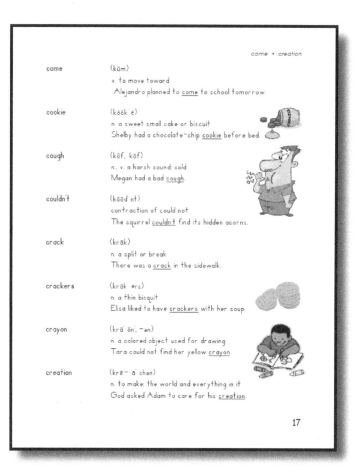

Correct Formation of Manuscript Letters and Numbers

Correct Formation of Cursive Letters and Numbers

Aa Bb Cc Dd Ee Ff

Gg Hh Ii Jj Kk

Ll Mm Nn Oo Pp

Qq Rr Ss Tt Uu

Vv Ww Xx Yy Zz

1 2 3 4 5 6 7 8 9 10

! ? . , : ; " " — ...

Scope & Sequence

Week 1

Lessons 1-5:

Goal: To review and study initial consonant blends: **cl, dr, fr, br.**

Week 2

Lessons 6-10:

Goal: To learn and study blends and diagraphs: **th, rd, ch, sh.**

Week 3

Lessons 11-15:

Goal: To recognize and spell words with the letter **r** after a vowel.

Week 4

Lessons 16-20:

Goal: To recognize and spell words with long and short **a** vowel sounds.

Week 5

Lessons 21-25:

Goal: To recognize and spell words with long and short **e** vowel sounds.

Week 6

Lessons 26-30:

Goal: To recognize and spell words with long and short **i** vowel sounds.

Week 7

Lessons 31-35:

Goal: To recognize and spell words with long and short **o** vowel sounds.

Week 8

Lessons 36-40:

Goal: To review words from Lessons 1-35.
Review the rules for the first seven weeks.

Week 9

Lessons 41-45:

Goal: To recognize and spell words with the **ô** sound.

Week 10

Lessons 46-50:

Goal: To recognize and spell words with a silent **e** after a long vowel sound.

Week 11

Lessons 51-55:

Goal: To recognize and spell words ending in **-ing.**

Week 12

Lessons 56-60:

Goal: To recognize and spell correctly words with regular plurals.

Week 13

Lessons 61-65:

Goal: To recognize and spell number words.

Week 14

Lessons 66-70:

Goal: To recognize and spell homonyms.

Week 15

Lessons 71-75:

Goal: To recognize and spell homonyms.

Week 16

Lessons 76-80:

Goal: To review words from Lessons 41-75.
Review all rules used in the last seven weeks.

Week 17

Lessons 81-85:

Goal: To recognize and spell words with the silent letter combinations **mb, kn, wr, qu, ck**.

Week 18

Lessons 86-90:

Goal: To recognize and spell words with the **ou** and **oi** sounds.

Week 19

Lessons 91-95:

Goal: To recognize and spell words with the **s** and **j** sounds.

Week 20

Lessons 96-100:

Goal: To recognize and spell words with the **ee** and **oo** sounds.

Week 21

Lessons 101-105:

Goal: To recognize and spell words with the **gh** letter combination.

Week 22

Lessons 106-110:

Goal: To recognize and spell words with irregular verb tenses.

Week 23

Lessons 111-115:

Goal: To recognize and spell words with the prefixes **un**, **re**, **dis**, and **pre**.

Week 24

Lessons 116-120:

Goal: To review spelling words from Lessons 81-115.
Review all rules used in the last seven weeks.

Week 25

Lessons 121-125:

Goal: To recognize and spell words ending in the suffixes **ly**, **ful**, and **ness**.

Week 26

Lessons 126-130:

Goal: To recognize and spell words with contractions.

Week 27

Lessons 131-135:

Goal: To recognize and spell words with multiple syllables.

Week 28

Lessons 136-140:

Goal: To recognize and spell words ending in -**ing** and -**ed**.

Week 29

Lessons 141-145:

Goal: To recognize and spell compound words.

Week 30

Lessons 146-150:

Goal: To recognize and spell words with **ea** vowel combinations.

Week 31

Lessons 151-155:

Goal: To recognize and spell words with the silent **e**.

Week 32

Lessons 156-160:

Goal: To review spelling words from Lessons 117-155.
Review all spelling rules.

Teacher Lessons

Week 1

Lessons 1-5 — Assess Student's Knowledge

Goal: To review and study the consonant blends: *cl, br, dr,* and *fr*.

Review rules:

In an *r* blend, two or more consonants come together in a word. Their sounds blend, but each sound is heard.
Examples: *brown, draw, from.*

In an *l* blend, two or more consonants come together in a word. Their sounds blend, but each sound is heard.
Examples: *clip* and *clean.*

What Do You Know?

Give the students the page from the *Student Book* for this lesson. Tell them that this page will be used to see what they currently know about the words for the week. Ask them to listen carefully to each word as you say it, repeat it in a sentence, and say it once again. Follow the procedures for this page as described in the Introduction at the beginning of this *Teacher's Guide*.

Show students how to write their assigned challenge words in the appropriate section at the back of their *Spelling Dictionary*.

Week 1 Worksheet Key

Lesson 1
Introduce Words

Activities:

1. Give the students the page from the *Student Book* for this lesson.

2. Read to students the directions for the first activity on the sheet. Remind them that after they have unscrambled the letters, they need to underline the consonant blends. Go over the correct answers as a class.

3. Direct students in completing the second part of the activity sheet. Students should put the words in alphabetical order. You may want to remind them of what it means to put things in alphabetical order and write an example on the board. When students have completed their work, go over the correct answers. Students can then go on to put the challenge words in alphabetical order.

4. Instruct students to write their assigned challenge words in their *Spelling Dictionaries* in the back section. Words are to be written under the correct letter of the alphabet.

Extended Activities for the Week:

1. Send a list of the week's words home for additional study. You may want to include a letter to the parents urging them to help the students both study and use the words for each week. Emphasize the importance of using spelling words in sentences, in speech, in stories, etc. so that they are given a context and not simply memorized.

2. Challenge students to create lists of additional words with the l and r blend. They can look for words they encounter in their other subjects or in their free reading. Maybe some of the students' names have *l* or *r* blends.

3. Have students begin the writing of sentences for each spelling word in their notebooks.

4. Assign the reproducible *Week 1 Worksheet* either as homework or as an added classroom activity.

Lesson 2 – Examine and Explore Words

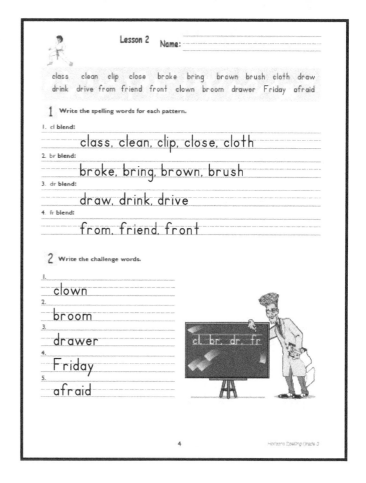

Teaching Tips:

1. Review the consonant blends students are working with for the week.

2. Have the class read the list of spelling words together with you.

Activities:

1. Give the students the page from the *Student Book* for this lesson.

2. Review the words in the word box as well as the challenge words.

3. Read the directions with the students and have them write the spelling word that fits each pattern.

4. On the board, write the letters of the blends: *cl, br, dr, fr*. Have students take turns coming to the board and writing words that fit under each of the blends. Emphasize the need to spell the words correctly.

5. Have students complete the worksheet where they write each of the challenge words.

6. Have students indicate the blend of each spelling word.

Extended Activities:

1. Ask students if they can think of other words that have the consonant blends highlighted in the spelling words of the week.

2. Have students continue writing the sentences for each spelling word in their notebooks.

Lesson 3 – Look at Context and Meaning of Words

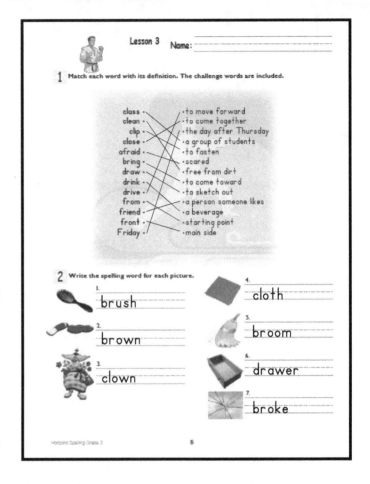

Teaching Tips:

1. Review words and rules.

2. Give students an opportunity to share any spelling word sentences they have written in their notebooks.

Activities:

1. Give the students the page from the *Student Book* for this lesson.

2. Read the directions on the activity sheet with the students. Have students match the spelling words with the definitions at the top of the page. When they have finished, review the answers as a class.

3. Have students complete the bottom half of the activity sheet. Go over those answers as well.

Extended Activities:

1. Ask students to choose two of the spelling words and draw pictures representing those words. Give an opportunity to share their pictures with the class.

2. Have students continue writing sentences for each spelling word in their notebooks.

3. Give students an opportunity to quiz each other on the spelling words and their definitions.

Horizons Spelling Grade 3

Lesson 4 – Apply Understanding of Words in Writing

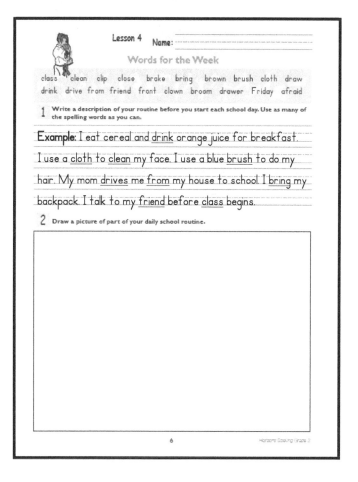

Activities:

1. Give the students the page from the *Student Book* for this lesson.

2. Read the directions for the first activity on the sheet.

3. As a class, brainstorm things students do before going to school. **Examples** may include *eating breakfast, making a bed, brushing teeth, riding a bus,* or *packing a lunch.* Tell students to look at the list of spelling words and think of ways they can fit those words into a story about getting ready for school. You may want to set as a goal using five spelling words in the writing exercise.

4. Direct students in drawing scenes from their morning routines.

Extended Activities:

1. Share stories.

2. Share pictures.

3. Have the students continue writing sentences for each spelling word in their notebooks.

Lesson 5 – Assess and Evaluate Progress

Activities:

1. Give the students the page from the *Student Book* for this lesson. Tell the students that this is a "Check-up" page to see what they have learned during the week. (Note: Teachers/parents of home schoolers may decide what will be assessed. If a student does exceptionally well on the "What do you know?" pre-assessment, the teacher may choose not to test words already known by the student. Or the teacher may choose to test all words for the week.)

2. Tell students that you will say a word and use it in a sentence. They will listen to the word and the sentence. Then, they will write the word on the line next to the numbers. All challenge words are included in this review.

3. Say the word. Repeat it in the context of a sentence. Repeat the word.

4. The students write the dictated word.

5. The process is repeated until all words have been tested.

6. The teacher may correct in class by writing the words on the board and having the students compare or "self-correct" their work. The teacher may also correct each student's work individually.

7. The teacher then writes any corrections for words misspelled in the space provided.

8. The students study the misspelled words, and practice them on the second side of the Lesson page.

9. Space is provided for retesting, for testing additional sight or "challenge words" added for the week, and for additional practice.

8

Lesson 5   Name:

Check up time

Spelling Test

1.   13.
2.   14.
3.   15.
4.   16.
5.   17.
6.   18.
7.   19.
8.   20.
9.   21.
10.   22.
11.   23.
12.   24.

Corrections

Horizons Spelling Grade 3   7

Extended Activity:

Review any words missed. Send words to review home for additional study. Encourage all students in their efforts.

Week 2

Lessons 6-10 — Assess Student's Knowledge

Goal: To review and study the consonant blends and diagraphs: *th, rd, ch,* and *sh.*

Review rules:

In an *r* blend, two or more consonants come together in a word.
Examples: *word* and *bird.*

A consonant diagraph is two or more consonants that stay together to make a special sound. In this lesson students will review the diagraphs *th, ch,* and *sh.* **Example:** *the, much, shall.*

What Do You Know?

Give the students the page from the *Student Book* for this lesson. Tell them that this page will be used to see what they currently know about the words for the week. Ask them to listen carefully to each word as you say it, repeat it in a sentence, and say it once again. Explain to them how in the previous lesson they learned about consonant blends. They will add a new one in this lesson: *rd.* Tell them the difference between a consonant blend and a consonant diagraph. Follow the procedures for this page as described in the Introduction at the beginning of this *Teacher's Guide.*

Show students how to write their assigned challenge words in the appropriate section at the back of their *Spelling Dictionary.*

Week 2 Worksheet Key

Lesson 6 – Introduce Words

Activities:

1. Give the students the page from the *Student Book* for this lesson.

2. Read to students the directions for the first activity on the sheet. Remind them of the blend and diagraphs they are studying in this lesson.

3. Ask students to find all the words with the *th* sound and write them on the sheet. Go over the answers with the class.

4. Have students find all the words with the *rd* blend and write them on the activity sheet. Ask students to share their answers when they have finished.

5. Next students should look for words with the diagraph *ch*. Review the correct answers with the class.

6. The final diagraph students need to find in words is *sh*. Once again go over the correct responses with the class.

7. Instruct students to write their assigned challenge words in their *Spelling Dictionaries* in the back section. Words are to be written under the correct letter of the alphabet.

Extended Activities for the Week:

1. Send a list of the week's words home for additional study. You may want to include a letter to the parents urging them to help the students both study and use the words for each week. Emphasize the importance of using spelling words in sentences, in speech, in stories, etc. so that they are given a context and not simply memorized.

2. Challenge students to create lists of additional words with the *rd* blend and the *th, ch,* and *sh* diagraphs. They can look for words they encounter in their other subjects or in their free reading. Maybe some of the students' names have an *rd* blend or *th, ch,* or *sh* diagraph.

3. Have students begin the writing of sentences for each spelling word in their notebooks.

4. Assign the reproducible *Week 2 Worksheet* either as homework or as an added classroom activity.

Horizons Spelling Grade 3

Lesson 7 – Examine and Explore Words

Teaching Tips:

1. Review the *rd* blend and consonant diagraphs the students are working with for the week.

2. Have the class read the list of spelling words together with you.

Activities:

1. Give the students the page from the *Student Book* for this lesson.

2. Direct students to the top part of the worksheet where they are asked to put two groups of words in alphabetical order. Once students have completed this section, go over the answers as a class.

3. Students should complete the first matching exercise. Students will be asked to match each of five words with its correct definition. Make time to go over the correct responses with the students.

4. Have students finish by completing the matching exercise for the challenge words. Again have them go over the correct answers.

Extended Activities:

1. Ask students to write the words in the matching parts of the exercise in alphabetical order.

2. Have students continue writing the sentences for each spelling word in their notebooks.

Lesson 8 – Look at Context and Meaning of Words

Teaching Tips:

1. Review words and rules.

2. Give students an opportunity to share any spelling word sentences they have written in their notebooks.

Activities:

1. Give the students the page from the *Student Book* for this lesson.

2. Read the directions on the activity sheet with the students. Have students fill in the blanks with the correct spelling words. When they have finished, review the answers as a class.

3. Have students complete the challenge word section of the activity sheet. Go over those answers as well.

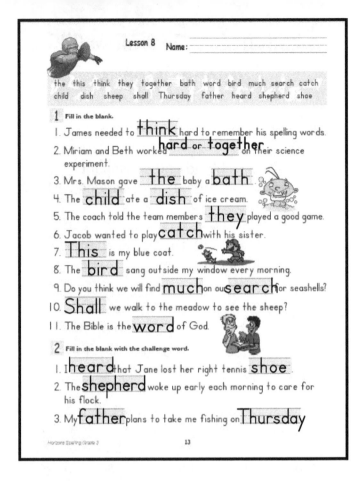

Extended Activities:

1. Ask students to choose two of the spelling words and draw pictures representing those words. Give an opportunity to share their pictures with the class.

2. Have students continue writing sentences for each spelling word in their notebooks.

3. Give students an opportunity to quiz each other on the spelling words and their definitions.

Lesson 9 – Apply Understanding of Words in Writing

Activities:

1. Give the students the page from the *Student Book* for this lesson.

2. Read the directions at the top of the activity sheet. You may want to brainstorm a list of things people can do and see at the zoo. Students can refer to this list as they write their sentences.

3. Direct students to draw a picture of one of their sentences in the space provided.

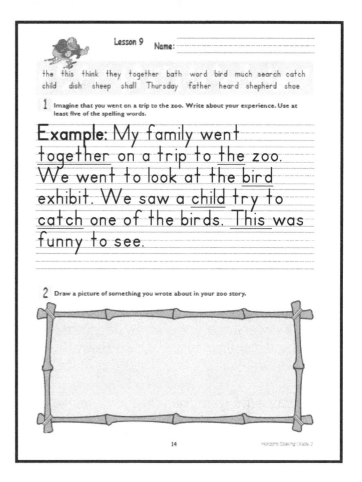

Extended Activities:

1. Share sentences.

2. Share drawings.

3. Have students work in pairs to see how many spelling words they can use in a single sentence.

4. Have students continue to write sentences for each spelling word in their notebooks.

Lesson 10 – Assess and Evaluate Progress

Activities:

1. Give the students the page from the *Student Book* for this lesson. Tell the students that this is a "Check-up" page to see what they have learned during the week. (Note: Teachers/parents of home schoolers may decide what will be assessed. If a student does exceptionally well on the "What do you know?" pre-assessment, the teacher may choose not to test words already known by the student. Or the teacher may choose to test all words for the week.)

2. Tell students that you will say a word and use it in a sentence. They will listen to the word and the sentence. Then, they will write the word on the line next to the numbers. All challenge words are included in this review.

3. Say the word. Repeat it in the context of a sentence. Repeat the word.

4. The students write the dictated word.

5. The process is repeated until all words have been tested.

6. The teacher may correct in class by writing the words on the board and having the students compare or "self-correct" their work. The teacher may also correct each student's work individually.

7. The teacher then writes any corrections for words misspelled in the space provided.

8. The students study the misspelled words, and practice them on the second side of the Lesson page.

9. Space is provided for retesting, for testing additional sight or "challenge words" added for the week, and for additional practice.

Check-up time   Lesson 10   Name:

Spelling Test

1.	13.
2.	14.
3.	15.
4.	16.
5.	17.
6.	18.
7.	19.
8.	20.
9.	21.
10.	22.
11.	23.
12.	24.

Corrections

Horizons Spelling Grade 3   15

Extended Activity:

Review any words missed. Send words to review home for additional study. Encourage all students in their efforts.

Week 3

Lessons 11-15 — Assess Student's Knowledge

Goal: To review and study words with the letter *r* after the vowel.

Review: Students should recognize the different sounds of vowels when an *r* follows.

Review Rules:
Remember that an *r* after a vowel makes a vowel sound different from a *short* or *long* sound. **Examples** include *warm, color,* and *were*.

What Do You Know?

Give the students the page from the *Student Book* for this lesson. Tell them that this page will be used to see what they currently know about the words for the week. Ask them to listen carefully to each word as you say it, repeat it in a sentence, and say it once again. Follow the procedures for this page as described in the Introduction at the beginning of this *Teacher's Guide*.

Show students how to write their assigned challenge words in the appropriate section at the back of their *Spelling Dictionary*.

Week 3 Worksheet Key

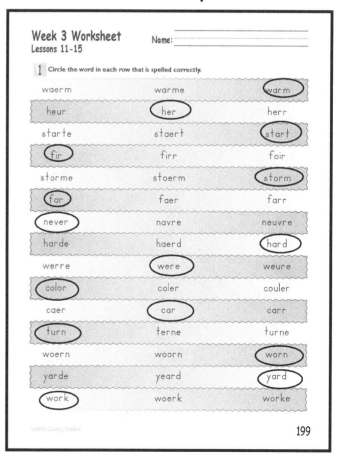

Lesson 11 – Introduce Words

Activities:

1. Give the students the page from the *Student Book* for this lesson.

2. Read to students the directions for the first activity on the sheet. Students will need to put all the vocabulary words in the correct sections on the activity sheet. When students have completed their work, go over the correct answers. As an added challenge, you may want to ask students to alphabetize the words in each group.

3. Draw students' attention to the last section of the activity sheet. Students should underline the vowel *r* combinations. Go over the correct responses with the class.

4. Have students write their assigned challenge words in their *Spelling Dictionaries* in the back section. Words are to be written under the correct letter of the alphabet.

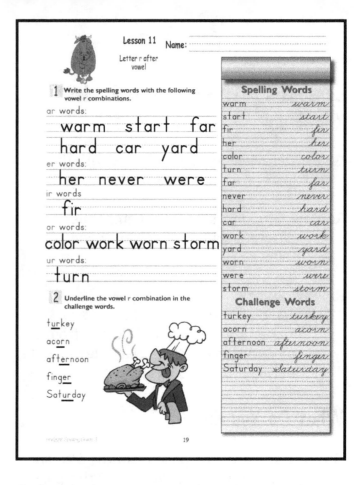

Extended Activities for the Week:

1. Send a list of the week's words home for additional study. You may want to include a letter to the parents urging them to help the students both study and use the words for each week. Emphasize the importance of using spelling words in sentences, in speech, in stories, etc. so that they are given a context and not simply memorized.

2. Challenge students to create lists of additional words that follow the vowel *r* pattern. They can look for words they encounter in their other subjects or in their free reading. Maybe some of the students' names have a vowel *r* pattern.

3. Have students begin the writing of sentences for each spelling word in their notebooks.

4. Assign the reproducible *Week 3 Worksheet* either as homework or as an added classroom activity.

Horizons Spelling Grade 3

Lesson 12 – Examine and Explore Words

Teaching Tips:

1. Review the vowel *r* words students are working with for the week.

2. Have the class read the list of spelling words together with you.

Activities:

1. Give the students the page from the *Student Book* for this lesson.

2. Review the rules for putting words in alphabetical order.

3. Read the directions at the top of the sheet with the students have them write the spelling words in alphabetical order. Go over the correct answers.

4. Go on to have students match the pictures with the correct spelling words.

5. Have students complete the worksheet by writing the challenge words in alphabetical order.

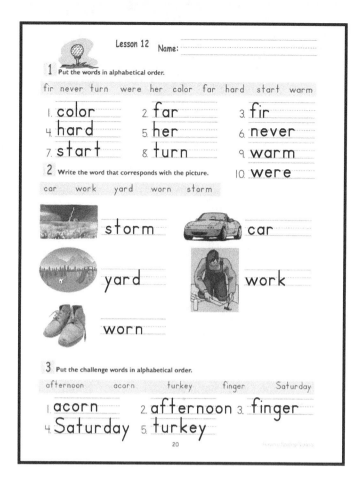

Extended Activities:

1. Ask students if they can think of other words that have the vowel *r* combinations highlighted in the spelling words of the week.

2. Have students continue writing the sentences for each spelling word in their notebooks.

Lesson 13 - Look at Context and Meaning of Words

Teaching Tips:

1. Review words and rules.

2. Give students an opportunity to share any spelling word sentences they have written in their notebooks.

Activities:

1. Give the students the page from the *Student Book* for this lesson.

2. Read the directions at the top of the page. Students will need to choose the correct spelling word for each sentence. When they have finished, review the answers as a class.

3. Have students complete the bottom half of the activity sheet. Here students will be asked to fill in the blanks with the correct challenge words. You may want to read through the list of challenge words before students begin. Go over those answers as well.

Extended Activities:

1. Direct students to write sentences for the spelling words that were not used in the sentences on the activity sheet.

2. Ask students to choose two of the spelling words and draw pictures representing those words. Give an opportunity to share their pictures with the class.

3. Have students continue writing sentences for each spelling word in their notebooks.

4. Give students an opportunity to quiz each other on the spelling words and their definitions.

Lesson 14 - Apply Understanding of Words in Writing

Activities:

1. Give the students the page from the *Student Book* for this lesson.

2. Read the directions for the first activity on the sheet. Discuss the two pictures with the students noting details in each. Ask the students to write about one of the pictures using as many spelling words as they can. Challenge them to use at least five spelling words in their descriptions.

3. Have students turn to the bottom activity on the sheet. Students will be asked to draw a picture representing one of the challenge words.

Extended Activities:

1. Share stories.

2. Share pictures.

3. Have students continue writing sentences for each spelling word in their notebooks.

Lesson 15 – Assess and Evaluate Progress

Activities:

1. Give the students the page from the *Student Book* for this lesson. Tell the students that this is a "Check-up" page to see what they have learned during the week. (Note: Teachers/parents of home schoolers may decide what will be assessed. If a student does exceptionally well on the "What do you know?" pre-assessment, the teacher may choose not to test words already known by the student. Or the teacher may choose to test all words for the week.)

2. Tell students that you will say a word and use it in a sentence. They will listen to the word and the sentence. Then, they will write the word on the line next to the numbers. All challenge words are included in this review.

3. Say the word. Repeat it in the context of a sentence. Repeat the word.

4. The students write the dictated word.

5. The process is repeated until all words have been tested.

6. The teacher may correct in class by writing the words on the board and having the students compare or "self-correct" their work. The teacher may also correct each student's work individually.

7. The teacher then writes any corrections for words misspelled in the space provided.

8. The students study the misspelled words, and practice them on the second side of the Lesson page.

9. Space is provided for retesting, for testing additional sight or "challenge words" added for the week, and for additional practice.

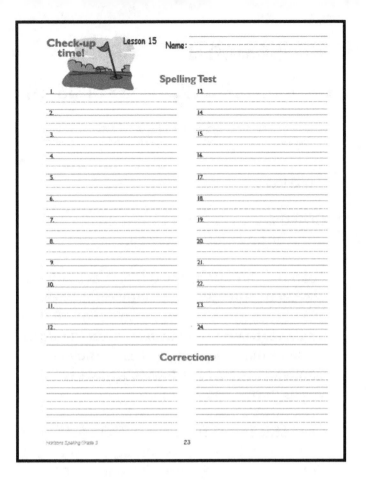

Extended Activity:

Review any words missed. Send words to review home for additional study. Encourage all students in their efforts.

Week 4

Lessons 16-20 — Assess Student's Knowledge

Goal: To recognize and spell words with the long *a* sound. To recognize and spell words with the short *a* sound.

Review rules:

Short Vowel Rule: When a word or syllable has only one vowel and it comes between two consonants, or at the beginning of the word or syllable, the vowel is usually short.

Long Vowel Rule: When a word or syllable has two vowels, the first vowel is usually long and the second vowel is usually silent. This includes the use of the letter *y* which is sometimes a vowel.

What Do You Know?

Give the students the page from the *Student Book* for this lesson. Tell them that this page will be used to see what they currently know about the words for the week. Ask them to listen carefully to each word as you say it, repeat it in a sentence, and say it once again. Follow the procedures for this page as described in the Introduction at the beginning of this *Teacher's Guide*.

Show students how to write their assigned challenge words in the appropriate section at the back of their *Spelling Dictionary*.

Week 4 Worksheet Key

Lesson 16 – Introduce Words

Activities:

1. Give the students the page from the *Student Book* for this lesson.

2. Ask students to look at the directions at the top of the page. Read through the word list with the students.

3. Direct students to complete the first section on the page where they identify words with the long *a* sound spelled *ay*. You may want to do one together and then have students complete the rest on their own. Go over the correct answers with the class.

4. Next have students identify words with the long *a* sound spelled *ai*. Go over the correct response with the class.

5. The final word with a long *a* sound will fit in the category of -*a-e*. Have students identify the word which fits this category.

6. Go on to have students identify the spelling words with the short *a* sound. You may want to complete one together as a class. When students have finished, have them take turns reading words that have the short *a* sound.

7. Instruct students to write their assigned challenge words in their *Spelling Dictionaries* in the back section. Words are to be written under the correct letter of the alphabet.

Extended Activities for the Week:

1. Send a list of the week's words home for additional study. You may want to include a letter to the parents urging them to help the students both study and use the words for each week. Emphasize the importance of using spelling words in sentences, in speech, in stories, etc. so that they are given a context and not simply memorized.

2. Have students write the definitions of the challenge words in their notebooks.

3. Have the students begin the writing of sentences for each spelling word in their notebooks.

4. Ask students to look for words with the long *a* sound to share in the next spelling class.

5. Assign the reproducible *Week 4 Worksheet* either as homework or as an added classroom activity.

Horizons Spelling Grade 3

Lesson 17 – Examine and Explore Words

Teaching Tips:

1. At the beginning of the class period, read with students the list of spelling words. You may want to exaggerate the long and short *a* sounds as you read.

2. Give students an opportunity to orally quiz each other on the spelling words.

Activities:

1. Give the students the page from the *Student Book* for this lesson.

2. Read through the directions at the top of the page.

3. Remind students that not all of the spelling words are a part of the crossword puzzle. They will need to choose the best word that fits both the clue and the spaces provided.

4. Go over the correct answers with the students.

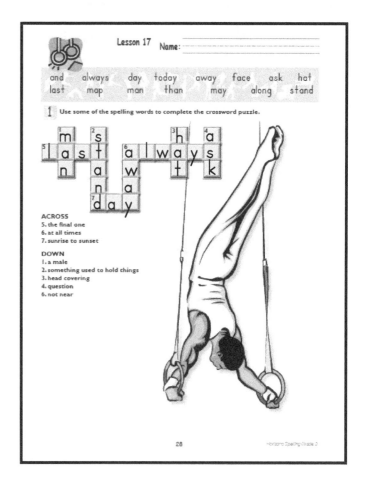

Extended Activities:

1. Ask students to come up with words that rhyme with the spelling words that end with a long *a* sound in the last syllable. For **example**: *trail* and *pail*; *face* and *space*; *day* and *stay*.

2. Have students continue writing the sentences for each spelling word in their notebooks.

Lesson 18 - Look at Context and Meaning of Words

Teaching Tips:

1. Review words and rules.

2. Give students an opportunity to share any spelling word sentences they have written in their notebooks.

Activities:

1. Give the students the page from the *Student Book* for this lesson.

2. Together read through the list of spelling words at the top of the page.

3. Have students complete the first section and then go over the answers as a class.

4. Direct students in completing the challenge word section at the bottom of the page. Once they have completed this section, go over the correct responses.

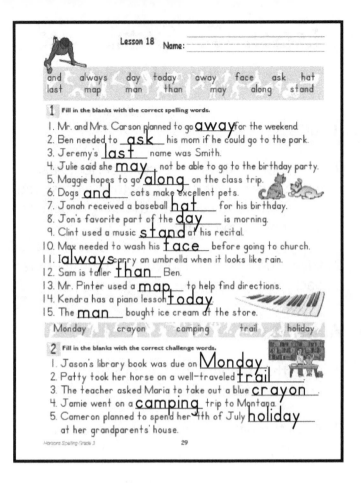

Extended Activities:

1. Have students finger spell the words in shaving cream or finger paint. They can wipe the shaving cream or paint smooth and go on to write the next spelling word.

2. Have students continue writing sentences for each spelling word in their notebooks.

3. Give students an opportunity to quiz each other on the spelling words and their definitions.

Lesson 19 – Apply Understanding of Words in Writing

Activities:

1. Give the students the page from the *Student Book* for this lesson.

2. Students should also take out their Bibles (KJV).

3. Read through the directions at the top of the page. Make sure students have their Bibles available to copy the appropriate Bible passages. If your students do not have KJV Bibles then prepare and duplicate the needed verses on a handout sheet.

4. After students have written the Bible verses and underlined the spelling words, go over the answers with the class.

Extended Activities:

1. Ask students to find additional words with long and short *a* sounds in the Bible passages they wrote on their worksheets.

2. Have the students continue writing sentences for each spelling word in their notebooks.

Lesson 20 – Assess and Evaluate Progress

Activities:

1. Give the students the page from the *Student Book* for this lesson. Tell the students that this is a "Check-up" page to see what they have learned during the week. (Note: Teachers/parents of home schoolers may decide what will be assessed. If a student does exceptionally well on the "What do you know?" pre-assessment, the teacher may choose not to test words already known by the student. Or the teacher may choose to test all words for the week.)

2. Tell students that you will say a word and use it in a sentence. They will listen to the word and the sentence. Then, they will write the word on the line next to the numbers. All challenge words are included in this review.

3. Say the word. Repeat it in the context of a sentence. Repeat the word.

4. The students write the dictated word.

5. The process is repeated until all words have been tested.

6. The teacher may correct in class by writing the words on the board and having the students compare or "self-correct" their work. The teacher may also correct each student's work individually.

7. The teacher then writes any corrections for words misspelled in the space provided.

8. The students study the misspelled words, and practice them on the second side of the Lesson page.

9. Space is provided for retesting, for testing additional sight or "challenge words" added for the week, and for additional practice.

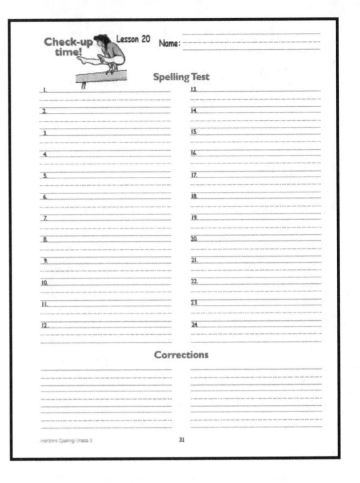

Extended Activity:

Review any words missed. Send words to review home for additional study. Encourage all students in their efforts.

Week 5

Lessons 21-25 — Assess Student's Knowledge

Goal: To review and study words with long and short *e* sounds.

Review rules:

When a word or syllable has only one vowel *e* and it comes between two consonants, or at the beginning of the word or syllable, the vowel is usually short. **Examples:** *every, best, spell.*

When a word or syllable has two vowels, the first vowel is usually long and the second vowel is usually silent. **Examples:** *read, freed, agree.*

When a word or syllable has just one vowel and the vowel comes at the end of the word or syllable, the vowel sound is usually long. **Examples:** *be, Jesus, every.*

What Do You Know?

Give the students the page from the *Student Book* for this lesson. Tell them that this page will be used to see what they currently know about the words for the week. Ask them to listen carefully to each word as you say it, repeat it in a sentence, and say it once again. Follow the procedures for this page as described in the Introduction at the beginning of this *Teacher's Guide*.

Show students how to write their assigned challenge words in the appropriate section at the back of their *Spelling Dictionary*.

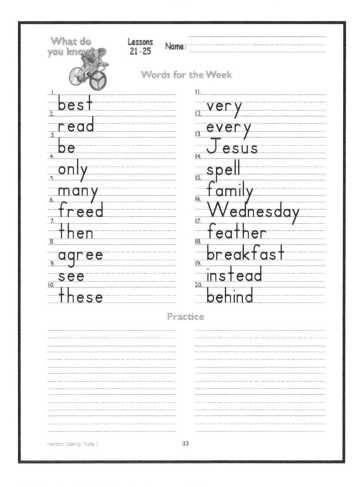

Week 5 Worksheet Key

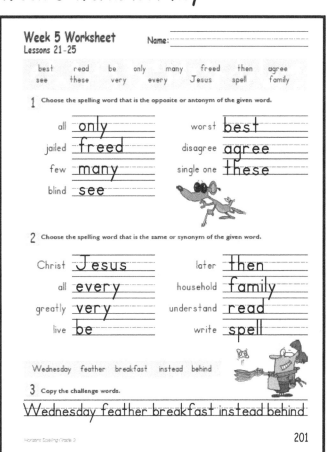

Lesson 21 - Introduce Words

Activities:

1. Give the students the page from the *Student Book* for this lesson.

2. Read to students the directions for the first activity on the sheet. After they have completed the activity, go over the correct answers as a class.

3. Direct students in completing the second part of the activity sheet. After they have completed the activity, go over the correct answers as a class.

4. Instruct students to write their assigned challenge words in their *Spelling Dictionaries* in the back section. Words are to be written under the correct letter of the alphabet.

Extended Activities for the Week:

1. Send a list of the week's words home for additional study. You may want to include a letter to the parents urging them to help the students both study and use the words for each week. Emphasize the importance of using spelling words in sentences, in speech, in stories, etc. so that they are given a context and not simply memorized.

2. Challenge students to create lists of additional words with long and short *e* sounds. They can look for words they encounter in their other subjects or in their free reading. Maybe some of the students' names have long or short *e* sounds.

3. Have students begin the writing of sentences for each spelling word in their notebooks.

4. Assign the reproducible *Week 5 Worksheet* either as homework or as an added classroom activity.

Horizons Spelling Grade 3

Lesson 22 – Examine and Explore Words

Teaching Tips:

1. Review long and short *e* sounds students are working with for the week.

2. Have the class read the list of spelling words together with you.

Activities:

1. Give the students the page from the *Student Book* for this lesson.

2. Review the words in the word box as well as the challenge words.

3. Read the directions with the students at the top of the page. Once they have completed this section, go over the answers with the class.

4. Direct students to complete the next activity on the sheet. When completed, go over the correct answers with the class.

5. Have students complete the activity sheet with the challenge words activity. Again, go over the correct responses with the class.

Extended Activities:

1. Ask students if they can think of other words that have long or short *e* sounds highlighted in the spelling words of the week.

2. Have students continue writing the sentences for each spelling word in their notebooks.

Lesson 23 – Look at Context and Meaning of Words

Teaching Tips:

1. Review words and rules.

2. Give students an opportunity to share any spelling word sentences they have written in their notebooks.

Activities:

1. Give the students the page from the *Student Book* for this lesson.

2. Read the directions on the top of the activity sheet with the students. When they have finished, review the answers as a class.

3. Have students complete the bottom half of the activity sheet. If needed, review the rules for alphabetical order. The challenge words are a part of this section. Go over those answers as well.

Extended Activities:

1. Ask students to choose two of the spelling words and draw pictures representing those words. Give an opportunity to share their pictures with the class.

2. Have students continue writing sentences for each spelling word in their notebooks.

3. Give students an opportunity to quiz each other on the spelling words and their definitions.

Lesson 24 – Apply Understanding of Words in Writing

Activities:

1. Give the students the page from the *Student Book* for this lesson.

2. Read the directions for the activity on the sheet. As a class, you may want to brainstorm possible sentences for the first grouping of words.

3. After students have finished the activity, give them an opportunity to share their sentences with the class.

Lesson 24 Name: _____

1 Use three of the four spelling words to write a sentence. Draw a picture to go along with the sentence.

1. read   these   every   Jesus
Ex: Every day my family reads a story about Jesus.

2. best   many   very   spell
Ex: Many of the best basketball players practice very hard.

3. agree   be   see   family
Ex: I will be able to see my family this summer.

38   Horizons Spelling Grade 3

Extended Activities:

1. Share pictures.

2. Have the students continue writing sentences for each spelling word in their notebooks.

Lesson 25 – Assess and Evaluate Progress

Activities:

1. Give the students the page from the *Student Book* for this lesson. Tell the students that this is a "Check-up" page to see what they have learned during the week. (Note: Teachers/parents of home schoolers may decide what will be assessed. If a student does exceptionally well on the "What do you know?" pre-assessment, the teacher may choose not to test words already known by the student. Or the teacher may choose to test all words for the week.)

2. Tell students that you will say a word and use it in a sentence. They will listen to the word and the sentence. Then, they will write the word on the line next to the numbers. All challenge words are included in this review.

3. Say the word. Repeat it in the context of a sentence. Repeat the word.

4. The students write the dictated word.

5. The process is repeated until all words have been tested.

6. The teacher may correct in class by writing the words on the board and having the students compare or "self-correct" their work. The teacher may also correct each student's work individually.

7. The teacher then writes any corrections for words misspelled in the space provided.

8. The students study the misspelled words, and practice them on the second side of the Lesson page.

9. Space is provided for retesting, for testing additional sight or "challenge words" added for the week, and for additional practice.

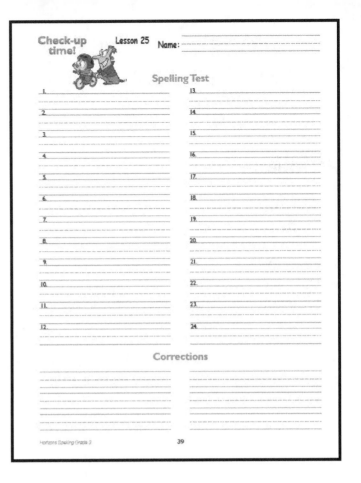

Extended Activity:

Review any words missed. Send words to review home for additional study. Encourage all students in their efforts.

Week 6

Lessons 26-30 — Assess Student's Knowledge

Goal: To review and study words with the long *i* and short *i* sounds.

Review rules:

When a word or syllable has only one vowel *i* and it comes between two consonants, or at the beginning of the word or syllable, the vowel is usually short. **Examples:** *his, big, if*.

When a word or syllable has two vowels, the first vowel is usually long and the second vowel is usually silent. **Examples:** *like and white*.

The letter combination *igh* sounds *i* and the letter *y* sometimes sounds *i*.

What Do You Know?

Give the students the page from the *Student Book* for this lesson. Tell them that this page will be used to see what they currently know about the words for the week. Ask them to listen carefully to each word as you say it, repeat it in a sentence, and say it once again. Follow the procedures for this page as described in the Introduction at the beginning of this *Teacher's Guide*.

Show students how to write their assigned challenge words in the appropriate section at the back of their *Spelling Dictionary*.

Week 6 Worksheet Key

Lesson 26 – Introduce Words

Activities:

1. Give the students the page from the *Student Book* for this lesson.

2. Read to students the directions for the first activity on the sheet. Go over the correct answers with the class.

3. Direct students in completing the second part of the activity sheet. Go over the correct answers with the class. As an added activity, ask the class to put the words in alphabetical order.

4. Instruct students to write their assigned challenge words in their *Spelling Dictionaries* in the back section. Words are to be written under the correct letter of the alphabet.

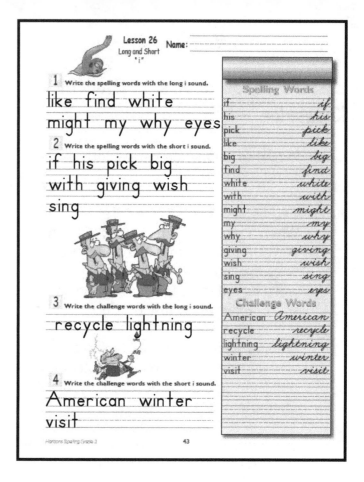

Extended Activities for the Week:

1. Send a list of the week's words home for additional study. You may want to include a letter to the parents urging them to help the students both study and use the words for each week. Emphasize the importance of using spelling words in sentences, in speech, in stories, etc. so that they are given a context and not simply memorized.

2. Challenge students to create lists of additional words with long and short *i* sounds. They can look for words they encounter in their other subjects or in their free reading. Maybe some of the students' names have long or short *i* sounds.

3. Have students begin the writing of sentences for each spelling word in their notebooks.

4. Assign the reproducible *Week 6 Worksheet* either as homework or as an added classroom activity.

Lesson 27 - Examine and Explore Words

Teaching Tips:

1. Review the long and short *i* vowel sounds students are working with for the week.

2. Have the class read the list of spelling words together with you.

Activities:

1. Give the students the page from the *Student Book* for this lesson.

2. Review the words in the word box as well as the challenge words.

3. Read the directions with the students. At the top of the sheet, students need to find words that rhyme with the spelling words on the list. Go over the correct responses with the class.

4. Direct students in completing the bottom part of the activity sheet. Go over those correct answers as well.

Extended Activities:

1. Ask students if they can think of other words that have long and short *i* sounds highlighted in the spelling words of the week.

2. Have students continue writing the sentences for each spelling word in their notebooks.

Lesson 28 – Look at Context and Meaning of Words

Teaching Tips:

1. Review words and rules.

2. Give students an opportunity to share any spelling word sentences they have written in their notebooks.

Activities:

1. Give the students the page from the *Student Book* for this lesson.

2. Read the directions on the activity sheet with the students. When they have finished, read the paragraphs as a class. Students may take turns reading each sentence.

Extended Activities:

1. Ask students to choose two of the spelling words and draw pictures representing those words. Give an opportunity to share their pictures with the class.

2. Have students continue writing sentences for each spelling word in their notebooks.

3. Give students an opportunity to quiz each other on the spelling words and their definitions.

Lesson 29 – Apply Understanding of Words in Writing

Activities:

1. Give the students the page from the *Student Book* for this lesson. Students should have their KJV Bibles available for the lesson.

2. Read the directions for the first activity on the sheet. Direct students in looking up the Bible verses. If your students do not have KJV Bibles then prepare and duplicate the needed verses on a handout sheet. You may want to have students complete this part with a partner.

3. Have students complete the bottom half of the activity sheet individually. You may want to have students share their words of praise.

Extended Activities:

1. Have the students continue writing sentences for each spelling word in their notebooks.

2. Ask students to find other Bible verses which contain some of their spelling words.

Lesson 30 – Assess and Evaluate Progress

Activities:

1. Give the students the page from the *Student Book* for this lesson. Tell the students that this is a "Check-up" page to see what they have learned during the week. (Note: Teachers/parents of home schoolers may decide what will be assessed. If a student does exceptionally well on the "What do you know?" pre-assessment, the teacher may choose not to test words already known by the student. Or the teacher may choose to test all words for the week.)

2. Tell students that you will say a word and use it in a sentence. They will listen to the word and the sentence. Then, they will write the word on the line next to the numbers. All challenge words are included in this review.

3. Say the word. Repeat it in the context of a sentence. Repeat the word.

4. The students write the dictated word.

5. The process is repeated until all words have been tested.

6. The teacher may correct in class by writing the words on the board and having the students compare or "self-correct" their work. The teacher may also correct each student's work individually.

7. The teacher then writes any corrections for words misspelled in the space provided.

8. The students study the misspelled words, and practice them on the second side of the Lesson page.

9. Space is provided for retesting, for testing additional sight or "challenge words" added for the week, and for additional practice.

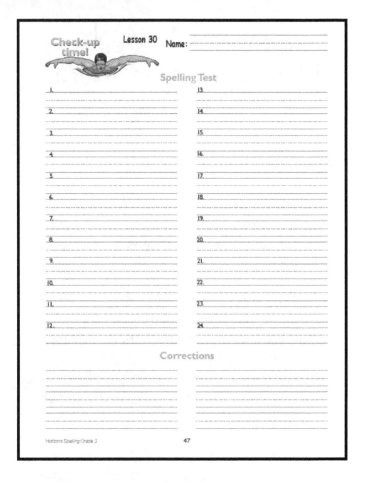

Extended Activity:

Review any words missed. Send words to review home for additional study. Encourage all students in their efforts.

Week 7

Lessons 31-35 — Assess Student's Knowledge

Goal: To review and study words with long and short vowel sounds.

Review rules:

When a word or syllable has only one vowel and it comes between two consonants, or at the beginning of the word or syllable, the vowel is usually short. **Examples:** *hot, add, in, on,* and *odd.*

When a word or syllable has two vowels, the first vowel is usually long and the second vowel is usually silent. **Examples:** *goes* and *coat.*

When a word or syllable has just one vowel, and the vowel comes at the end of the word or syllable, the vowel sound is usually long. **Examples:** *ago, echo, no, be, he, we, she,* and *dry.*

When vowels *i* and *o* are followed by two consonants they may say long *i* and long *o*. **Examples:** *find, old, wild, colt, kind, find, pint, both, post.* These are sometimes called Wild Colt Words.

What Do You Know?

Give the students the page from the *Student Book* for this lesson. Tell them that this page will be used to see what they currently know about the words for the week. Ask them to listen carefully to each word as you say it, repeat it in a sentence, and say it once again. Follow the procedures for this page as described in the Introduction at the beginning of this *Teacher's Guide*.

Show students how to write their assigned challenge words in the appropriate section at the back of their *Spelling Dictionary*.

Lessons 31-35   Name: _____

What do you know?

Words for the Week

1. grow
2. long
3. old
4. open
5. those
6. hot
7. both
8. goes
9. most
10. coat
11. soak
12. God
13. ago
14. owner
15. roll
16. Jehovah
17. volleyball
18. orange
19. toast
20. collar

Practice

Horizons Spelling Grade 3   49

Week 7 Worksheet Key

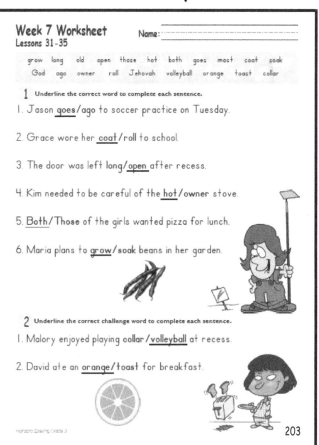

Week 7 Worksheet   Name: _____
Lessons 31-35

grow   long   old   open   those   hot   both   goes   most   coat   soak
God   ago   owner   roll   Jehovah   volleyball   orange   toast   collar

1 Underline the correct word to complete each sentence.

1. Jason <u>goes</u>/ago to soccer practice on Tuesday.

2. Grace wore her <u>coat</u>/roll to school.

3. The door was left long/<u>open</u> after recess.

4. Kim needed to be careful of the <u>hot</u>/owner stove.

5. <u>Both</u>/Those of the girls wanted pizza for lunch.

6. Maria plans to <u>grow</u>/soak beans in her garden.

2 Underline the correct challenge word to complete each sentence.

1. Malory enjoyed playing collar/<u>volleyball</u> at recess.

2. David ate an <u>orange</u>/toast for breakfast.

Horizons Spelling Grade 3   203

Lesson 31 - Introduce Words

Activities:

1. Give the students the page from the *Student Book* for this lesson.

2. Read to students the directions for the first activity on the sheet. Go over the correct answers with the students. You may want to emphasize the long *o* sound as you read through the list.

3. Direct students in completing the second part of the activity sheet. Go over the short *o* sounds as well.

4. Read to students the directions for the third activity on the sheet. You may want to emphasize the long *o* sound as you read through the challenge words. Go over the correct answers with the students.

5. Direct students in completing the fourth part of the activity sheet. Go over the short *o* challenge word sounds as well. The word *orange* is in this category since the pronunciation key gives it either a controlled *r* or a short *o* sound.

6. Instruct students to write their assigned challenge words in their *Spelling Dictionaries* in the back section. Words are to be written under the correct letter of the alphabet.

Extended Activities for the Week:

1. Send a list of the week's words home for additional study. You may want to include a letter to the parents urging them to help the students both study and use the words for each week. Emphasize the importance of using spelling words in sentences, in speech, in stories, etc. so that they are given a context and not simply memorized.

2. Challenge students to create lists of additional words with long and short *o* sounds. They can look for words they encounter in their other subjects or in their free reading. Maybe some of the students' names have long or short *o* sounds.

3. Have students begin the writing of sentences for each spelling word in their notebooks.

4. Assign the reproducible *Week 7 Worksheet* either as homework or as an added classroom activity.

Lesson 32 – Examine and Explore Words

Teaching Tips:

1. Review long and short *o* sounds that students are working with for the week.

2. Have the class read the list of spelling words together with you.

Activities:

1. Give the students the page from the *Student Book* for this lesson.

2. Review the words in the word box as well as the challenge words.

3. Read the directions with the students. Point out that they need to put the underlined letters in the blanks at the bottom of the page.

4. Go over the correct answers as well as the phrase at the bottom of the page.

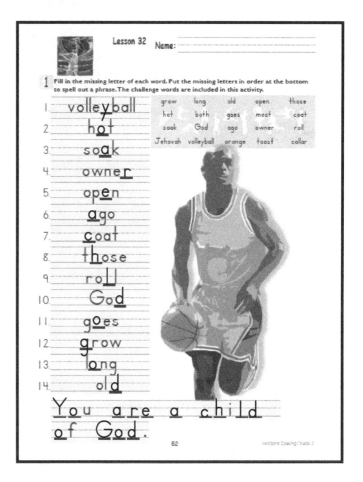

Extended Activities:

1. Ask students if they can think of other words that have the long and short *o* sounds highlighted in the spelling words of the week.

2. Have students continue writing the sentences for each spelling word in their notebooks.

Lesson 33 – Look at Context and Meaning of Words

Teaching Tips:

1. Review words and rules.

2. Give students an opportunity to share any spelling word sentences they have written in their notebooks.

Activities:

1. Give the students the page from the *Student Book* for this lesson.

2. Read the directions on the activity sheet with the students. When they have finished, review the answers as a class.

3. Have students complete the challenge word section. Go over those answers with the class.

Lesson 33   Name: _____

1 Put a *C* next to the sentence if the spelling word is used correctly in the sentence. Put a *W* next to the sentence if the use of the spelling word is wrong.

1. Hannah put the old fruit in the fridge. **W**
2. Ben locked the open door. **W**
3. Those book on the table are mine. **W**
4. The owner of the coat was Liz. **C**
5. Matthew and Tom goes to the same church. **W**
6. Jenny plans to grow her hair long. **C**
7. Katie ate most of her supper. **C**
8. The hot weather meant the swimming pool was open. **C**
9. The shirt needed to soak before it was washed. **C**
10. Both dog is mine. **W**
11. A long time ago, Michael wants to become a teacher. **W**

2 Put a *C* next to the sentence if the challenge word is used correctly in the sentence. Put a *W* next to the sentence if the use of the challenge word is wrong.

1. Jehovah is another name for God. **C**
2. Becky caught the volleyball in her glove. **W**
3. Carlos loves orange juice for breakfast. **C**
4. The collar of Duncan's shoe was missing. **W**
5. Clint wore toast on his feet to keep them warm. **W**

53

Extended Activities:

1. Ask students to choose two of the spelling words and draw pictures representing those words. Give an opportunity to share their pictures with the class.

2. Have students continue writing sentences for each spelling word in their notebooks.

3. Give students an opportunity to quiz each other on the spelling words and their definitions.

Lesson 34 – Apply Understanding of Words in Writing

Activities:

1. Give the students the page from the *Student Book* for this lesson.

2. Read the directions for the writing activity on the sheet.

3. As a class, go over the story of Joseph and his coat of many colors. You may find it helpful to write on the board the names of some of the key people in the story such as Joseph and Jacob. You may also want to write locations such as Egypt or Canaan on the board.

4. Direct students in writing their paragraphs and drawing accompanying pictures.

Extended Activities:

1. Share stories.

2. Share pictures.

3. Have the students continue writing sentences for each spelling word in their notebooks.

Lesson 35 – Assess and Evaluate Progress

Activities:

1. Give the students the page from the *Student Book* for this lesson. Tell the students that this is a "Check-up" page to see what they have learned during the week. (Note: Teachers/parents of home schoolers may decide what will be assessed. If a student does exceptionally well on the "What do you know?" pre-assessment, the teacher may choose not to test words already known by the student. Or the teacher may choose to test all words for the week.)

2. Tell students that you will say a word and use it in a sentence. They will listen to the word and the sentence. Then, they will write the word on the line next to the numbers. All challenge words are included in this review.

3. Say the word. Repeat it in the context of a sentence. Repeat the word.

4. The students write the dictated word.

5. The process is repeated until all words have been tested.

6. The teacher may correct in class by writing the words on the board and having the students compare or "self-correct" their work. The teacher may also correct each student's work individually.

7. The teacher then writes any corrections for words misspelled in the space provided.

8. The students study the misspelled words, and practice them on the second side of the Lesson page.

9. Space is provided for retesting, for testing additional sight or "challenge words" added for the week, and for additional practice.

Extended Activity:

Review any words missed. Send words to review home for additional study. Encourage all students in their efforts.

Check-up time!

Lesson 35   Name: _____

Spelling Test

1.	13.
2.	14.
3.	15.
4.	16.
5.	17.
6.	18.
7.	19.
8.	20.
9.	21.
10.	22.
11.	23.
12.	24.

Corrections

Horizons Spelling Grade 3   55

Week 8 - Skill Review

Lessons 36-40 — Once Again for Excellence

Goal: To review words from Lessons 1-35.

Review rules:
Review the rules for Weeks 1-7.

Teacher's Note:

Students will review 28 words each day from the previous seven weeks. All of the words from the previous weeks will be reviewed. None of the challenge words will be reviewed. Students should know that only 28 words will appear on the final test that are taken from Weeks 1-7.

What Do You Remember?

Give the students the page from the *Student Book* for this lesson. Tell them that this page will be used to see what they currently know about the review. Ask them to listen carefully to each word as you say it, repeat it in a sentence, and say it once again. Follow the procedures for this page as described in the Introduction at the beginning of this *Teacher's Guide*. Tell students that the challenge words will not be a part of the review.

Week 8 Worksheet Key

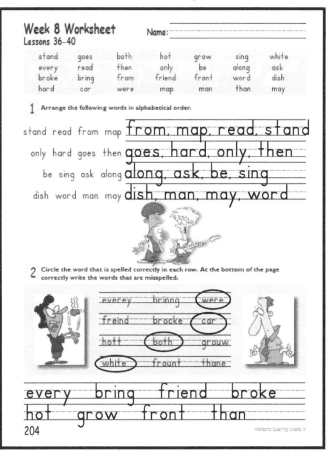

Lesson 36 – Practice Makes Perfect

Activities:

1. Give the students the page from the *Student Book* for this lesson.

2. Read to students the directions for the first activity on the sheet. Go over the answers for each of the categories on the top of the sheet.

3. Direct students in completing the second part of the activity sheet. Go over the sentences with the students.

Extended Activities for the Week:

1. Let parents know you will be reviewing spelling words this week. You may want to include a letter to the parents urging them to help the students both study and use the words from the previous seven weeks. Emphasize the importance of using spelling words in sentences, in speech, in stories, etc. so that they are given a context and not simply memorized.

2. Assign the reproducible *Week 8 Worksheet* either as homework or as an added classroom activity.

3. Make a chart categorizing the different words students have learned in the pervious seven weeks.

4. You may want to give students spot quizzes to check their spelling of the review words. Emphasize that these quizzes are not graded but are being used to help them review.

Lesson 37 – Revisit for Success

Activities:

1. Give the students the page from the *Student Book* for this lesson.

2. Review the words in the word box.

3. Read the directions with the students. You may want to have students first solve the clues before writing the words in the crossword puzzle. Go over the correct answers with the students.

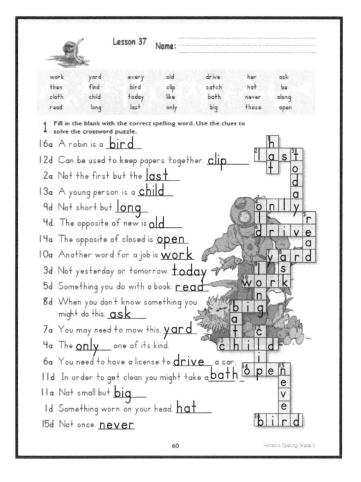

Extended Activities:

1. Check for any difficulties students are having with the review words.

2. You may want to give students spot quizzes to check their spelling of the review words. Emphasize that these quizzes are not graded but are being used to help them review.

Lesson 38 – Become an Expert

Activities:

1. Give the students the page from the *Student Book* for this lesson.

2. Read the directions on the activity sheet with the students. Remind students of the meaning of the word antonym. You may want to complete the first one together as a class. When they have finished, review the answers as a class.

3. Have students complete the second half of the activity sheet. Remind students of the meaning of the word synonym. You may want to complete the first one together as a class. Go over those answers as well.

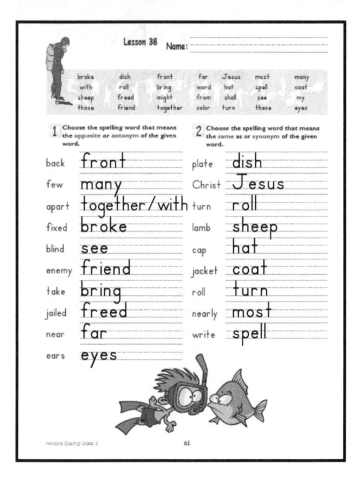

Extended Activities:

1. Ask students to choose two of the spelling words and draw pictures representing those words. Give an opportunity to share their pictures with the class.

2. Ask students to choose three of the spelling words and write sentences for them.

3. Give students an opportunity to quiz each other on the spelling words and their definitions.

4. You may want to give students spot quizzes to check their spelling of the review words. Emphasize that these quizzes are not graded but are being used to help them review.

Lesson 39 – Exercise for Mastery

Activities:

1. Give the students the page from the *Student Book* for this lesson.

2. Read the directions for the activity on the sheet.

3. As a class, brainstorm types of activities students do in art class. Brainstorm as well scenes students could draw in class.

4. You may want to give students an opportunity to share their sentences with the class.

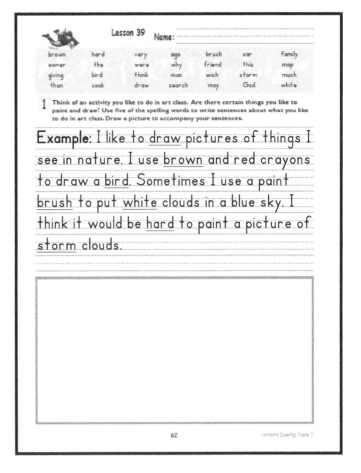

Extended Activities:

1. Share stories.

2. Share pictures.

3. Have the students continue writing sentences for each spelling word in their notebooks.

4. You may want to give students spot quizzes to check their spelling of the review words. Emphasize that these quizzes are not graded but are being used to help them review.

Lesson 40 – Assess and Evaluate

Activities:

1. Give the students the page from the *Student Book* for this lesson. Tell the students that this is a "Check-up" page to see what they have learned over the past seven weeks.

2. Tell students that you will say a word and use it in a sentence. They will listen to the word and the sentence. Then, they will write the word on the line next to the numbers.

3. Say the word. Repeat it in the context of a sentence. Repeat the word.

4. The students write the dictated word.

5. The process is repeated until all words have been tested.

6. The teacher may correct in class by writing the words on the board and having the students compare or "self-correct" their work. The teacher may also correct each student's work individually.

7. The teacher then writes any corrections for words misspelled in the space provided.

8. The students study the misspelled words, and practice them on the second side of the Lesson page.

Words for the final test:

warm	start	for
word	storm	catch
child	her	never
many	freed	see
these	Jesus	spell
owner	be	only
then	read	every
most	eyes	might
color	yard	ago
coat		

Extended Activity:

Review any words missed. Encourage all students in their efforts.

Week 9

Lessons 41-45 — Assess Student's Knowledge

Goal: To review and study words with the ô sound.

Review rules:
The ô sound can be spelled *a, au, aw* or *w*. **Examples** include *small, sauce, straw,* and *naughty*.

What Do You Know?

Give the students the page from the *Student Book* for this lesson. Tell them that this page will be used to see what they currently know about the words for the week. Ask them to listen carefully to each word as you say it, repeat it in a sentence, and say it once again. Follow the procedures for this page as described in the Introduction at the beginning of this *Teacher's Guide*.

Show students how to write their assigned challenge words in the appropriate section at the back of their *Spelling Dictionary*.

Week 9 Worksheet Key

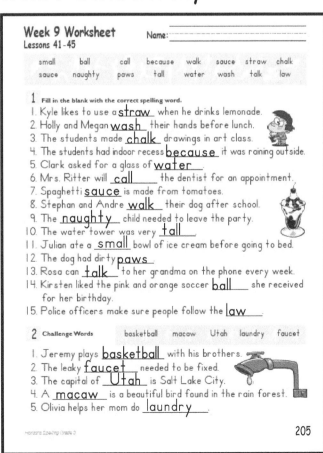

Lesson 41 – Introduce Words

Activities:

1. Give the students the page from the *Student Book* for this lesson.

2. Read to students the directions for the activity on the sheet.

3. Students will be asked to arrange the spelling words based on their spelling of the ô sound.

4. Instruct students to write their assigned challenge words in their *Spelling Dictionaries* in the back section. Words are to be written under the correct letter of the alphabet.

Extended Activities for the Week:

1. Send a list of the week's words home for additional study. You may want to include a letter to the parents urging them to help the students both study and use the words for each week. Emphasize the importance of using spelling words in sentences, in speech, in stories, etc. so that they are given a context and not simply memorized.

2. Challenge students to create lists of additional words with ô sounds. They can look for words they encounter in their other subjects or in their free reading. Maybe some of the students' names have ô.

3. Have students begin the writing of sentences for each spelling word in their notebooks.

4. Assign the reproducible *Week 9 Worksheet* either as homework or as an added classroom activity.

Lesson 42 – Examine and Explore Words

Teaching Tips:

1. Review the ô sound students are working with for the week.

2. Have the class read the list of spelling words together with you.

Activities:

1. Give the students the page from the *Student Book* for this lesson.

2. Students will be asked to identify the misspelled word in each sentence.

3. You can extend the activity by having students write the misspelled words and the correctly spelled words on a sheet of paper.

Extended Activities:

1. Ask students if they can think of other words that have ô sound highlighted in the spelling words of the week.

2. Students could write each spelling word three times. They should use different color crayons each time they write words.

3. Have students continue writing the sentences for each spelling word in their notebooks.

Lesson 43 – Look at Context and Meaning of Words

Activities:

1. Give the students the page from the *Student Book* for this lesson.

2. Read the directions on the activity sheet with the students. When they have finished, review the answers as a class.

3. Have students complete the challenge word section of the activity sheet. Go over those answers as well.

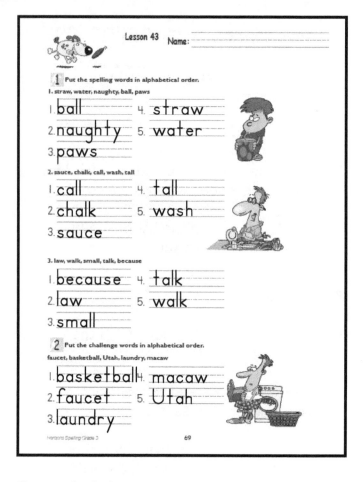

Extended Activities:

1. Ask students to choose two of the spelling words and draw pictures representing those words. Give an opportunity to share their pictures with the class.

2. Have students continue writing sentences for each spelling word in their notebooks.

3. Give students an opportunity to quiz each other on the spelling words and their definitions.

Horizons Spelling Grade 3

Lesson 44 – Apply Understanding of Words in Writing

Activities:

1. Give the students' the page from the *Student Book* for this lesson.

2. Read the directions for the first activity on the sheet.

3. Write four random spelling words on the board. As a class brainstorm possible sentences made from three of the four words.

4. Direct students in completing the activity sheet. Go over student's responses at the end of class.

Extended Activities:

1. Have students try to use five of the spelling words in one sentence. Tell them that it's fine if the sentence is silly.

2. Ask students to write each word forward and backward.

3. Have the students continue writing sentences for each spelling word in their notebooks.

Lesson 45 – Assess and Evaluate Progress

Activities:

1. Give the students the page from the *Student Book* for this lesson. Tell the students that this is a "Check-up" page to see what they have learned during the week. (Note: Teachers/parents of home schoolers may decide what will be assessed. If a student does exceptionally well on the "What do you know?" pre-assessment, the teacher may choose not to test words already known by the student. Or the teacher may choose to test all words for the week.)

2. Tell students that you will say a word and use it in a sentence. They will listen to the word and the sentence. Then, they will write the word on the line next to the numbers. All challenge words are included in this review.

3. Say the word. Repeat it in the context of a sentence. Repeat the word.

4. The students write the dictated word.

5. The process is repeated until all words have been tested.

6. The teacher may correct in class by writing the words on the board and having the students compare or "self-correct" their work. The teacher may also correct each student's work individually.

7. The teacher then writes any corrections for words misspelled in the space provided.

8. The students study the misspelled words, and practice them on the second side of the Lesson page.

9. Space is provided for retesting, for testing additional sight or "challenge words" added for the week, and for additional practice.

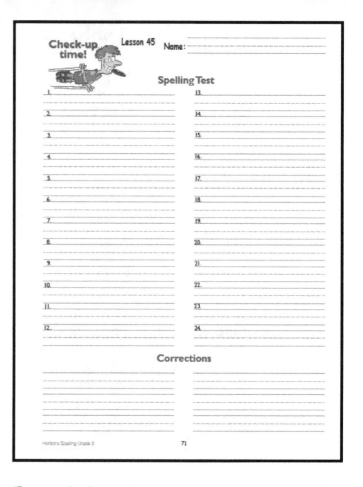

Extended Activity:

Review any words missed. Send words to review home for additional study. Encourage all students in their efforts.

Week 10

Lessons 46-50 — Assess Student's Knowledge

Goal: To review and study words with a silent *e* after a long vowel sound.

Review rules:
> A vowel is generally long if it is followed by a consonant plus a silent *e*. The exception is when the consonant is an *r*. **Examples** include *make* and *hive*.

What Do You Know?

Give the students the page from the *Student Book* for this lesson. Tell them that this page will be used to see what they currently know about the words for the week. Ask them to listen carefully to each word as you say it, repeat it in a sentence, and say it once again. Follow the procedures for this page as described in the Introduction at the beginning of this *Teacher's Guide*.

Show students how to write their assigned challenge words in the appropriate section at the back of their *Spelling Dictionary*.

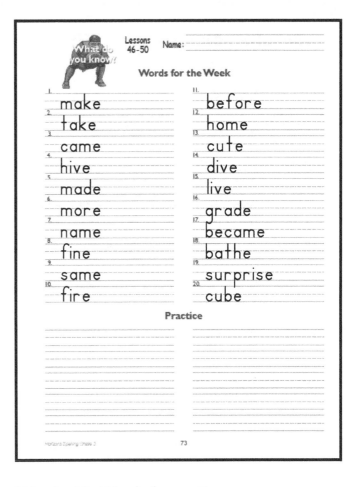

Week 10 Worksheet Key

Week 10 Worksheet
Lessons 46-50   Name: _____

1 Underline the correct word for each sentence.

1. Mr. Carson made a camp <u>fire</u>/dive for his family.

2. Jonah asked if he could name/<u>take</u> his dog for a walk.

3. Mrs. Hobart make/<u>made</u> a pumpkin pie last week.

4. The bee home/<u>hive</u> was a busy place.

5. Elliot asked for <u>more</u>/fine ice cream.

6. The mail <u>came</u>/before early yesterday.

2 Underline the correct challenge word for each sentence.

1. The caterpillar grade/<u>became</u> a butterfly.

2. Mrs. Foster planned to <u>bathe</u>/surprise her infant and wash her hair.

206   *Horizons Spelling Grade 3*

Lesson 46 – Introduce Words

Activities:

1. Give the students the page from the *Student Book* for this lesson.

2. Read to students the directions for the first activity on the sheet.

3. Direct students in completing the second part of the activity sheet.

4. Instruct students to write their assigned challenge words in their *Spelling Dictionaries* in the back section.

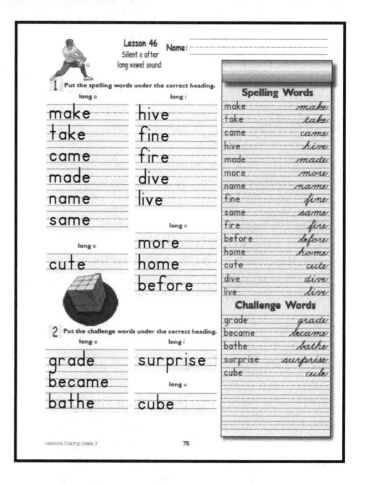

Extended Activities for the Week:

1. Send a list of the week's words home for additional study. You may want to include a letter to the parents urging them to help the students both study and use the words for each week. Emphasize the importance of using spelling words in sentences, in speech, in stories, etc. so that they are given a context and not simply memorized.

2. Challenge students to create lists of additional words with a silent *e* after a long vowel sound. They can look for words they encounter in their other subjects or in their free reading.

3. Have students begin the writing of sentences for each spelling word in their notebooks.

4. Assign the reproducible *Week 10 Worksheet* either as homework or as an added classroom activity.

Horizons Spelling Grade 3

Lesson 47 – Examine and Explore Words

Teaching Tips:

1. Review words students are working with for the week.

2. Have the class read the list of spelling words together with you.

Activities:

1. Give the students the page from the *Student Book* for this lesson.

2. Review the words in the word box as well as the challenge words.

3. Read the directions with the students.

4. When students have completed filling in the blanks, go over the correct answers with the class.

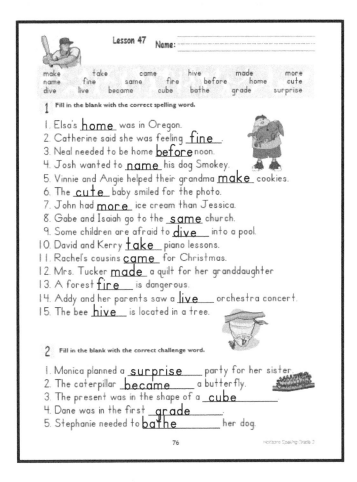

Extended Activities:

1. Ask students if they can think of other words that have a long vowel sound with a silent e highlighted in the spelling words of the week.

2. Students should write each of their spelling words replacing each consonant with a dash.

3. Have students continue writing the sentences for each spelling word in their notebooks.

Lesson 48 – Look at Context and Meaning of Words

Teaching Tips:

1. Review words and rules.

2. Give students an opportunity to share any spelling word sentences they have written in their notebooks.

Activities:

1. Give the students the page from the *Student Book* for this lesson.

2. Read the directions on the activity sheet with the students. When they have finished, review the answers as a class.

3. Have students complete the challenge words section on the activity sheet. Go over those answers as well.

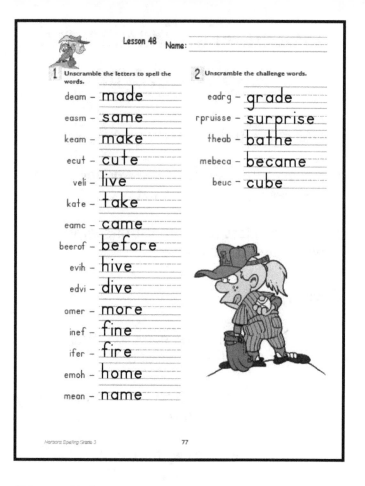

Extended Activities:

1. Ask students to choose two of the spelling words and draw pictures representing those words. Give an opportunity to share their pictures with the class.

2. Have students continue writing sentences for each spelling word in their notebooks.

3. Give students an opportunity to quiz each other on the spelling words and their definitions.

Lesson 49 – Apply Understanding of Words in Writing

Activities:

1. Give the students the page from the *Student Book* for this lesson.

2. Read the directions for the activity on the sheet.

3. As a class, brainstorm a possible spring or fall scene. This will give students an idea of how to complete the winter and summer scenes on the activity sheet.

4. Direct students in completing the activity.

Lesson 49   Name:

1   Draw a picture and write sentences for each scene. Try to use four spelling words in describing each scene.

1. A Winter Activity

Example: I like to make snowmen in front of our home. Sometimes we take time to make snow angels. Last year we made a snow fort.

2. A Summer Activity

Example: Last summer we went camping. My dad made a camp fire. Before bed I asked for one more s'more.

78   Horizons Spelling Grade 3

Extended Activities:

1. Share stories.

2. Share pictures.

3. Have the students continue writing sentences for each spelling word in their notebooks.

Lesson 50 – Assess and Evaluate Progress

Activities:

1. Give the students the page from the Student Book for this lesson. Tell the students that this is a "Check-up" page to see what they have learned during the week. (Note: Teachers/parents of home schoolers may decide what will be assessed. If a student does exceptionally well on the "What do you know?" pre-assessment, the teacher may choose not to test words already known by the student. Or the teacher may choose to test all words for the week.)

2. Tell students that you will say a word and use it in a sentence. They will listen to the word and the sentence. Then, they will write the word on the line next to the numbers. All challenge words are included in this review.

3. Say the word. Repeat it in the context of a sentence. Repeat the word.

4. The students write the dictated word.

5. The process is repeated until all words have been tested.

6. The teacher may correct in class by writing the words on the board and having the students compare or "self-correct" their work. The teacher may also correct each student's work individually.

7. The teacher then writes any corrections for words misspelled in the space provided.

8. The students study the misspelled words, and practice them on the second side of the Lesson page.

9. Space is provided for retesting, for testing additional sight or "challenge words" added for the week, and for additional practice.

Check-up Lesson 50   time!   Name:

Spelling Test

1.	13.
2.	14.
3.	15.
4.	16.
5.	17.
6.	18.
7.	19.
8.	20.
9.	21.
10.	22.
11.	23.
12.	24.

Corrections

Extended Activity:

Review any words missed. Send words to review home for additional study. Encourage all students in their efforts.

Week 11

Lessons 51-55 — Assess Student's Knowledge

Goal: To review and study words with *-ing* endings.

Review rules:

When adding the suffix *-ing*, the root word usually stays the same. **Examples:** *jumping* and *holding*.

When adding the suffix *-ing* to root words, drop the silent *e* before adding the suffix. **Examples:** *using* and *hiding*.

What Do You Know?

Give the students the page from the *Student Book* for this lesson. Tell them that this page will be used to see what they currently know about the words for the week. Ask them to listen carefully to each word as you say it, repeat it in a sentence, and say it once again. Follow the procedures for this page as described in the Introduction at the beginning of this *Teacher's Guide*.

Show students how to write their assigned challenge words in the appropriate section at the back of their *Spelling Dictionary*.

Week 11 Worksheet Key

Lesson 51 – Introduce Words

Activities:

1. Give the students the page from the *Student Book* for this lesson.

2. Review the rules for adding the suffix *-ing* to root words.

3. Read to students the directions for the activity on the sheet. Go over the answers and spellings as a class.

4. Direct students in completing the second part of the activity sheet.

5. Instruct students to write their assigned challenge words in their *Spelling Dictionaries* in the back section.

Extended Activities for the Week:

1. Send a list of the week's words home for additional study. You may want to include a letter to the parents urging them to help the students both study and use the words for each week. Emphasize the importance of using spelling words in sentences, in speech, in stories, etc. so that they are given a context and not simply memorized.

2. Challenge students to create lists of additional words with *-ing*. They can look for words they encounter in their other subjects or in their free reading.

3. Have students begin the writing of sentences for each spelling word in their notebooks.

4. Assign the reproducible *Week 11 Worksheet* either as homework or as an added classroom activity.

Lesson 52 - Examine and Explore Words

Teaching Tips:

1. Review the *–ing* words students are working with for the week.

2. Have the class read the list of spelling words together with you.

Activities:

1. Give the students the page from the *Student Book* for this lesson.

2. Read the directions with the students. Remind them they need to find the spelling words in the word search and write them at the bottom of the page.

3. Go over any words that may have been difficult for students to find.

Extended Activities:

1. Ask students if they can think of other words that have *–ing* highlighted in the spelling words of the week.

2. Have students continue writing the sentences for each spelling word in their notebooks.

Lesson 53 – Look at Context and Meaning of Words

Teaching Tips:

1. Review words and rules.

2. Give students an opportunity to share any spelling word sentences they have written in their notebooks.

Activities:

1. Give the students the page from the *Student Book* for this lesson.

2. Read the directions on the activity sheet with the students. You may want to go over the first question as a class.

3. When students have finished the activity, review the answers as a class.

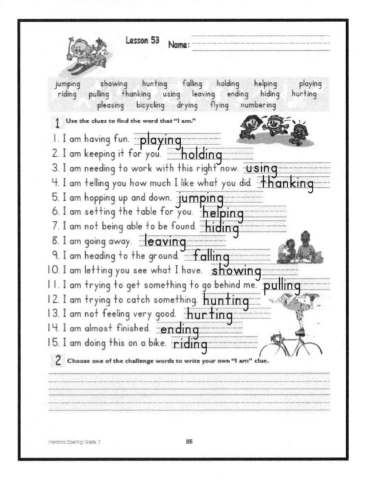

Extended Activities:

1. Ask students to choose two of the spelling words and draw pictures representing those words. Give an opportunity to share their pictures with the class.

2. Have students continue writing sentences for each spelling word in their notebooks.

3. Give students an opportunity to quiz each other on the spelling words and their definitions.

Lesson 54 – Apply Understanding of Words in Writing

Activities:

1. Give the students the page from the *Student Book* for this lesson.

2. Read the directions for the first activity on the sheet.

3. As a class, brainstorm pieces of equipment or games you might see on a playground.

4. Direct students in completing the activity sheet.

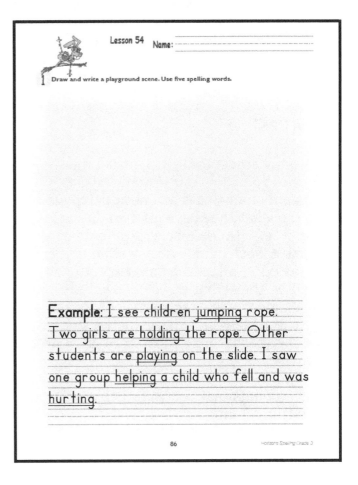

Lesson 54   Name: _____

Draw and write a playground scene. Use five spelling words.

Example: I see children jumping rope. Two girls are holding the rope. Other students are playing on the slide. I saw one group helping a child who fell and was hurting.

86   Horizons Spelling Grade 3

Extended Activities:

1. Share stories.

2. Share pictures.

3. Have the students continue writing sentences for each spelling word in their notebooks.

Lesson 55 – Assess and Evaluate Progress

Activities:

1. Give the students the page from the *Student Book* for this lesson. Tell the students that this is a "Check-up" page to see what they have learned during the week. (Note: Teachers/parents of home schoolers may decide what will be assessed. If a student does exceptionally well on the "What do you know?" pre-assessment, the teacher may choose not to test words already known by the student. Or the teacher may choose to test all words for the week.)

2. Tell students that you will say a word and use it in a sentence. They will listen to the word and the sentence. Then, they will write the word on the line next to the numbers. All challenge words are included in this review.

3. Say the word. Repeat it in the context of a sentence. Repeat the word.

4. The students write the dictated word.

5. The process is repeated until all words have been tested.

6. The teacher may correct in class by writing the words on the board and having the students compare or "self-correct" their work. The teacher may also correct each student's work individually.

7. The teacher then writes any corrections for words misspelled in the space provided.

8. The students study the misspelled words, and practice them on the second side of the Lesson page.

9. Space is provided for retesting, for testing additional sight or "challenge words" added for the week, and for additional practice.

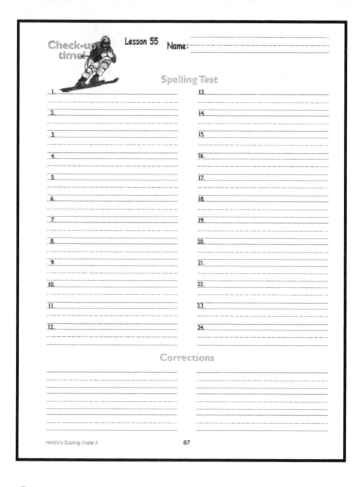

Extended Activity:

Review any words missed. Send words to review home for additional study. Encourage all students in their efforts.

Week 12

Lessons 56-60 — Assess Student's Knowledge

Goal: To review and study regular plurals.

Review rules:
Many plurals are formed by adding -*s* to the end of the word.
Examples include *girls* and *hands*.

If a word ends in *ss*, *x*, *ch* or *sh*, the suffix -*es* is added to from the plural. **Examples** include *dresses* and *washes*.

When a word ends in a -*y* after a consonant, the -*y* usually changes to an -*i* before adding -*es*. **Examples** include *city, cities, baby, babies, story, stories.*

What Do You Know?

Give the students the page from the *Student Book* for this lesson. Tell them that this page will be used to see what they currently know about the words for the week. Ask them to listen carefully to each word as you say it, repeat it in a sentence, and say it once again. Follow the procedures for this page as described in the Introduction at the beginning of this *Teacher's Guide*.

Show students how to write their assigned challenge words in the appropriate section at the back of their *Spelling Dictionary*.

Week 12 Worksheet Key

Lesson 56 - Introduce Words

Activities:

1. Give the students the page from the *Student Book* for this lesson.

2. Read to students the directions for the activity sheet.

3. Instruct students to write their assigned challenge words in their *Spelling Dictionaries* in the back section. Words are to be written under the correct letter of the alphabet.

Extended Activities for the Week:

1. Send a list of the week's words home for additional study. You may want to include a letter to the parents urging them to help the students both study and use the words for each week. Emphasize the importance of using spelling words in sentences, in speech, in stories, etc. so that they are given a context and not simply memorized.

2. Challenge students to create lists of additional words with -s and -es plural endings. They can look for words they encounter in their other subjects or in their free reading.

3. Have students begin the writing of sentences for each spelling word in their notebooks.

4. Assign the reproducible *Week 12 Worksheet* either as homework or as an added classroom activity.

Lesson 57 – Examine and Explore Words

Teaching Tips:

1. Review the plural words students are working with for the week.

2. Have the class read the list of spelling words together with you.

Activities:

1. Give the students the page from the *Student Book* for this lesson.

2. Review the words in the word box as well as the challenge words.

3. Read the directions with the students. When they have completed the activity, go over the correct answers as a class. You may want to have students take turns coming to the board and writing the spelling word correctly.

Extended Activities:

1. Ask students if they can think of other plural words.

2. Have students write their words using a cereal with alphabets.

3. Have students continue writing the sentences for each spelling word in their notebooks.

Lesson 58 – Look at Context and Meaning of Words

Teaching Tips:

1. Review words and rules.

2. Give students an opportunity to share any spelling word sentences they have written in their notebooks.

Activities:

1. Give the students the page from the *Student Book* for this lesson.

2. Read the directions at the top of the activity sheet with the students. When they have finished, review the answers as a class.

3. Ask students to complete the next section of the activity sheet which asks students to put the words in alphabetical order. Go over these answers together.

4. Have students complete the challenge word section of the activity sheet. Go over those answers as well.

Extended Activities:

1. Ask students to choose two of the spelling words and draw pictures representing those words. Give an opportunity to share their pictures with the class.

2. Have students continue writing sentences for each spelling word in their notebooks.

3. Give students an opportunity to quiz each other on the spelling words and their definitions.

Lesson 59 – Apply Understanding of Words in Writing

Activities:

1. Give the students the page from the *Student Book* for this lesson.

2. Read the directions for the activity on the sheet.

3. Have students describe some of the things they see in the picture.

4. Direct students in writing their descriptions.

Extended Activities:

1. Share stories.

2. Write your words on a computer using fun fonts.

3. Have the students continue writing sentences for each spelling word in their notebooks.

Lesson 60 - Assess and Evaluate Progress

Activities:

1. Give the students the page from the *Student Book* for this lesson. Tell the students that this is a "Check-up" page to see what they have learned during the week. (Note: Teachers/parents of home schoolers may decide what will be assessed. If a student does exceptionally well on the "What do you know?" pre-assessment, the teacher may choose not to test words already known by the student. Or the teacher may choose to test all words for the week.)

2. Tell students that you will say a word and use it in a sentence. They will listen to the word and the sentence. Then, they will write the word on the line next to the numbers. All challenge words are included in this review.

3. Say the word. Repeat it in the context of a sentence. Repeat the word.

4. The students write the dictated word.

5. The process is repeated until all words have been tested.

6. The teacher may correct in class by writing the words on the board and having the students compare or "self-correct" their work. The teacher may also correct each student's work individually.

7. The teacher then writes any corrections for words misspelled in the space provided.

8. The students study the misspelled words, and practice them on the second side of the Lesson page.

9. Space is provided for retesting, for testing additional sight or "challenge words" added for the week, and for additional practice.

Extended Activity:

Review any words missed. Send words to review home for additional study. Encourage all students in their efforts.

Week 13

Lessons 61-65 — Assess Student's Knowledge

Goal: To review and study the spelling of number words.

Review rules:
Students will spell the numbers one through ten. They will see the relationships between these "root" words and the words formed from them.

What Do You Know?

Give the students the page from the *Student Book* for this lesson. Tell them that this page will be used to see what they currently know about the words for the week. Ask them to listen carefully to each word as you say it, repeat it in a sentence, and say it once again. Follow the procedures for this page as described in the Introduction at the beginning of this *Teacher's Guide*.

Show students how to write their assigned challenge words in the appropriate section at the back of their *Spelling Dictionary*.

Week 13 Worksheet Key

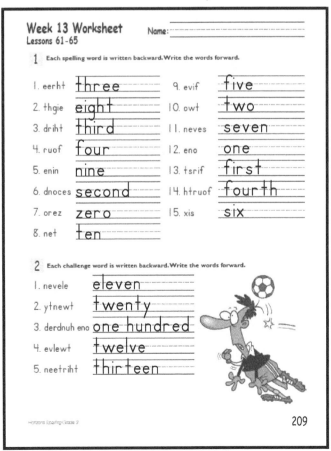

Lesson 61 – Introduce Words

Activities:

1. Give the students the page from the *Student Book* for this lesson.

2. Read to students the directions for the activity on the sheet. Go over the correct responses when students have finished.

3. You can extend the activity by having students write the misspelled words correctly on a sheet of paper.

4. Instruct students to write their assigned challenge words in their *Spelling Dictionary* in the back section. Words are to be written under the correct letter of the alphabet.

Extended Activities for the Week:

1. Send a list of the week's words home for additional study. You may want to include a letter to the parents urging them to help the students both study and use the words for each week. Emphasize the importance of using spelling words in sentences, in speech, in stories, etc. so that they are given a context and not simply memorized.

2. Challenge students to create lists of additional number words. They can look for words they encounter in their other subjects or in their free reading.

3. Have students begin the writing of sentences for each spelling word in their notebooks.

4. Assign the reproducible *Week 13 Worksheet* either as homework or as an added classroom activity.

Lesson 62 – Examine and Explore Words

Teaching Tips:

1. Review the words students are working with for the week.

2. Have the class read the list of spelling words together with you.

Activities:

1. Give the students the page from the *Student Book* for this lesson.

2. Review the words in the word box as well as the challenge words.

3. Read the directions with the students. Students will be asked to write out the spelling word for each numeral.

4. Go over the correct answers with the class.

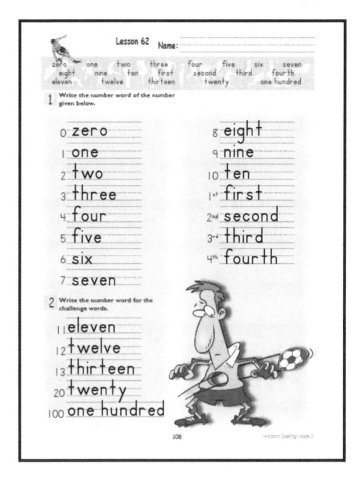

Extended Activities:

1. Have students continue writing the sentences for each spelling word in their notebooks.

Lesson 63 – Look at Context and Meaning of Words

Teaching Tips:

1. Review words and rules.

2. Give students an opportunity to share any spelling word sentences they have written in their notebooks.

Activities:

1. Give the students the page from the *Student Book* for this lesson.

2. Read the directions on the activity sheet with the students. When they have finished, review the answers as a class.

3. Have students complete the challenge word section of the activity sheet. Go over those answers as well.

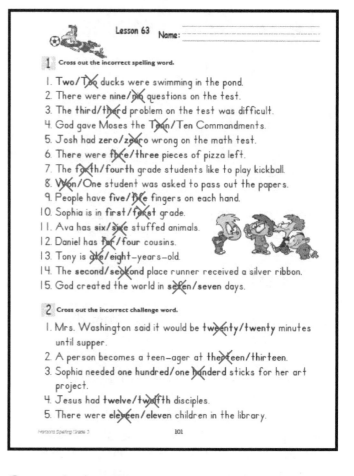

Extended Activities:

1. Ask students to choose two of the spelling words and draw pictures representing those words. Give an opportunity to share their pictures with the class.

2. Have students continue writing sentences for each spelling word in their notebooks.

3. Give students an opportunity to quiz each other on the spelling words and their definitions.

Lesson 64 – Apply Understanding of Words in Writing

Activities:

1. Give the students the page from the *Student Book* for this lesson.

2. Read the directions for the activity on the sheet.

3. As a class, brainstorm general information about homes and apartments that would involve numbers.

4. Direct students in drawing pictures and writing sentences.

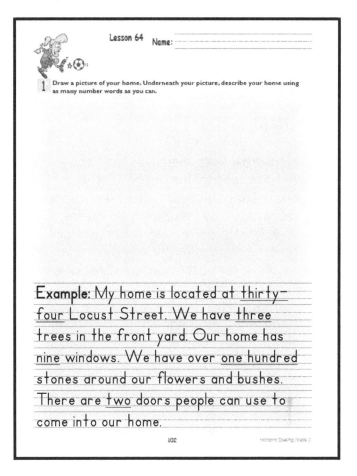

Lesson 64   Name: _____

1 Draw a picture of your home. Underneath your picture, describe your home using as many number words as you can.

Example: My home is located at thirty-four Locust Street. We have three trees in the front yard. Our home has nine windows. We have over one hundred stones around our flowers and bushes. There are two doors people can use to come into our home.

102   Horizons Spelling Grade 3

Extended Activities:

1. Write down your phone number. After writing down the numerals, spell your phone number.

2. Share pictures.

3. Have the students continue writing sentences for each spelling word in their notebooks.

Lesson 65 - Assess and Evaluate Progress

Activities:

1. Give the students the page from the *Student Book* for this lesson. Tell the students that this is a "Check-up" page to see what they have learned during the week. (Note: Teachers/parents of home schoolers may decide what will be assessed. If a student does exceptionally well on the "What do you know?" pre-assessment, the teacher may choose not to test words already known by the student. Or the teacher may choose to test all words for the week.)

2. Tell students that you will say a word and use it in a sentence. They will listen to the word and the sentence. Then, they will write the word on the line next to the numbers. All challenge words are included in this review.

3. Say the word. Repeat it in the context of a sentence. Repeat the word.

4. The students write the dictated word.

5. The process is repeated until all words have been tested.

6. The teacher may correct in class by writing the words on the board and having the students compare or "self-correct" their work. The teacher may also correct each student's work individually.

7. The teacher then writes any corrections for words misspelled in the space provided.

8. The students study the misspelled words, and practice them on the second side of the Lesson page.

9. Space is provided for retesting, for testing additional sight or "challenge words" added for the week, and for additional practice.

Lesson 65   Name: _____

Check-up time!

Spelling Test

1.	13.
2.	14.
3.	15.
4.	16.
5.	17.
6.	18.
7.	19.
8.	20.
9.	21.
10.	22.
11.	23.
12.	24.

Corrections

Horizons Spelling Grade 3   103

Extended Activity:

Review any words missed. Send words to review home for additional study. Encourage all students in their efforts.

Week 14

Lessons 66-70 — Assess Student's Knowledge

Goal: To review and study homonyms.

Review rules:
> Homonyms are words that sound alike but have different spellings and meanings.

What Do You Know?

Give the students the page from the *Student Book* for this lesson. Tell them that this page will be used to see what they currently know about the words for the week. Ask them to listen carefully to each word as you say it, repeat it in a sentence, and say it once again. Follow the procedures for this page as described in the Introduction at the beginning of this *Teacher's Guide*.

Show students how to write their assigned challenge words in the appropriate section at the back of their *Spelling Dictionary*.

Week 14 Worksheet Key

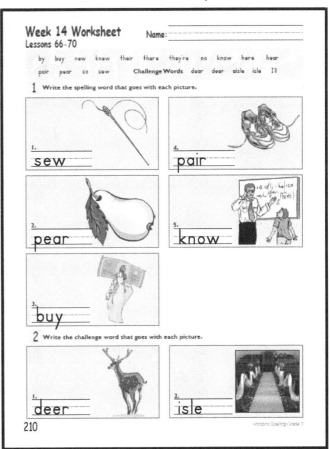

Lesson 66 – Introduce Words

Activities:

1. Give the students the page from the *Student Book* for this lesson.

2. Read to students the directions for the first activity on the sheet. Go over the correct answers with the class. As an added challenge, ask students to provide sentences for the "wrong" answers.

3. Direct students in completing the second part of the activity sheet.

4. Instruct students to write their assigned challenge words in their *Spelling Dictionaries* in the back section. Words are to be written under the correct letter of the alphabet.

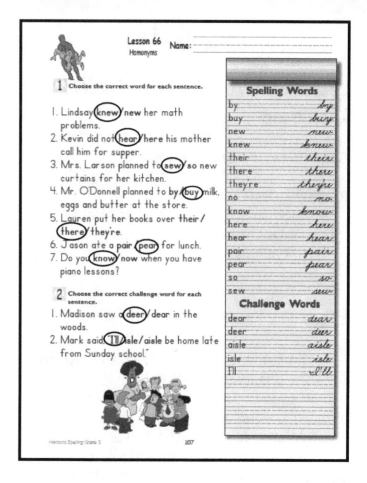

Extended Activities for the Week:

1. Send a list of the week's words home for additional study. You may want to include a letter to the parents urging them to help the students both study and use the words for each week. Emphasize the importance of using spelling words in sentences, in speech, in stories, etc. so that they are given a context and not simply memorized.

2. Challenge students to create lists of additional homonyms. They can look for words they encounter in their other subjects or in their free reading.

3. Have students begin the writing of sentences for each spelling word in their notebooks.

4. Assign the reproducible *Week 14 Worksheet* either as homework or as an added classroom activity.

Lesson 67 - Examine and Explore Words

Teaching Tips:

1. Review the homonyms students are working with for the week.

2. Have the class read the list of spelling words together with you.

Activities:

1. Give the students the page from the *Student Book* for this lesson.

2. Read the directions with the students.

3. Go over the correct answers with the class.

4. Have students finish by completing the challenge word section.

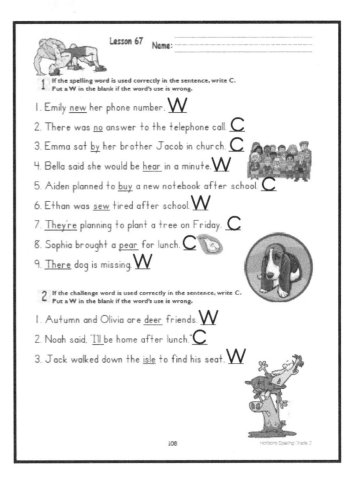

Lesson 67   Name: _____

1 If the spelling word is used correctly in the sentence, write C.
Put a W in the blank if the word's use is wrong.

1. Emily <u>new</u> her phone number. **W**
2. There was <u>no</u> answer to the telephone call. **C**
3. Emma sat <u>by</u> her brother Jacob in church. **C**
4. Bella said she would be <u>hear</u> in a minute. **W**
5. Aiden planned to <u>buy</u> a new notebook after school. **C**
6. Ethan was <u>sew</u> tired after school. **W**
7. <u>They're</u> planning to plant a tree on Friday. **C**
8. Sophia brought a <u>pear</u> for lunch. **C**
9. <u>There</u> dog is missing. **W**

2 If the challenge word is used correctly in the sentence, write C.
Put a W in the blank if the word's use is wrong.

1. Autumn and Olivia are <u>deer</u> friends. **W**
2. Noah said, "<u>I'll</u> be home after lunch." **C**
3. Jack walked down the <u>isle</u> to find his seat. **W**

108   Horizons Spelling Grade 3

Extended Activities:

1. Ask students if they can think of other homonyms.

2. Have students continue writing the sentences for each spelling word in their notebooks.

Lesson 68 – Look at Context and Meaning of Words

Teaching Tips:

1. Review words and rules.

2. Give students an opportunity to share any spelling word sentences they have written in their notebooks.

Activities:

1. Give the students the page from the *Student Book* for this lesson.

2. Read the directions on the activity sheet with the students. When they have finished, review the answers as a class.

3. Have students complete the bottom half of the activity sheet. Go over those answers as well.

Extended Activities:

1. Ask students to choose two of the spelling words and draw pictures representing those words. Give an opportunity to share their pictures with the class.

2. Have students continue writing sentences for each spelling word in their notebooks.

3. Give students an opportunity to quiz each other on the spelling words and their definitions.

Lesson 69 – Apply Understanding of Words in Writing

Activities:

1. Give the students the page from the *Student Book* for this lesson.

2. Read the directions for the activity on the sheet.

3. As a class, brainstorm funny ways of using either the homonyms on the word list or other homonyms.

4. Direct students in writing the sentences and drawing accompanying pictures.

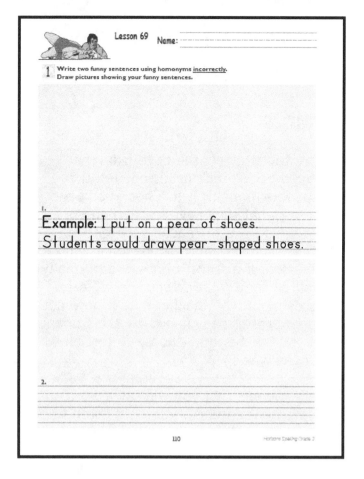

Lesson 69   Name: _____

1 Write two funny sentences using homonyms *incorrectly*.
Draw pictures showing your funny sentences.

1.

Example: I put on a pear of shoes.
Students could draw pear-shaped shoes.

2.

110   Horizons Spelling Grade 3

Extended Activities:

1. Share sentences.

2. Share pictures.

3. Have the students continue writing sentences for each spelling word in their notebooks.

Lesson 70 – Assess and Evaluate Progress

Activities:

1. Give the students the page from the *Student Book* for this lesson. Tell the students that this is a "Check-up" page to see what they have learned during the week. (Note: Teachers/parents of home schoolers may decide what will be assessed. If a student does exceptionally well on the "What do you know?" pre-assessment, the teacher may choose not to test words already known by the student. Or the teacher may choose to test all words for the week.)

2. Tell students that you will say a word and use it in a sentence. They will listen to the word and the sentence. Then, they will write the word on the line next to the numbers. All challenge words are included in this review.

3. Say the word. Repeat it in the context of a sentence. Repeat the word.

4. The students write the dictated word.

5. The process is repeated until all words have been tested.

6. The teacher may correct in class by writing the words on the board and having the students compare or "self-correct" their work. The teacher may also correct each student's work individually.

7. The teacher then writes any corrections for words misspelled in the space provided.

8. The students study the misspelled words, and practice them on the second side of the Lesson page.

9. Space is provided for retesting, for testing additional sight or "challenge words" added for the week, and for additional practice.

Check-up time!   Lesson 70   Name:

Spelling Test

1.   13.
2.   14.
3.   15.
4.   16.
5.   17.
6.   18.
7.   19.
8.   20.
9.   21.
10.   22.
11.   23.
12.   24.

Corrections

Horizons Spelling Grade 3   111

Extended Activity:

Review any words missed. Send words to review home for additional study. Encourage all students in their efforts.

Week 15

Lessons 71-75 — Assess Student's Knowledge

Goal: To review and study homonyms.

Review rules:
> Homonyms are words that sound alike but have different spellings and meanings.

What Do You Know?

Give the students the page from the *Student Book* for this lesson. Tell them that this page will be used to see what they currently know about the words for the week. Ask them to listen carefully to each word as you say it, repeat it in a sentence, and say it once again. Follow the procedures for this page as described in the Introduction at the beginning of this *Teacher's Guide*.

Show students how to write their assigned challenge words in the appropriate section at the back of their *Spelling Dictionary*.

Week 15 Worksheet Key

Lesson 71 – Introduce Words

Activities:

1. Give the students the page from the Student Book for this lesson.

2. Read to students the directions for the first activity on the sheet. Go over the correct answers with the class.

3. Direct students in completing the challenge word section of the activity sheet.

4. Instruct students to write their assigned challenge words in their *Spelling Dictionaries* in the back section. Words are to be written under the correct letter of the alphabet.

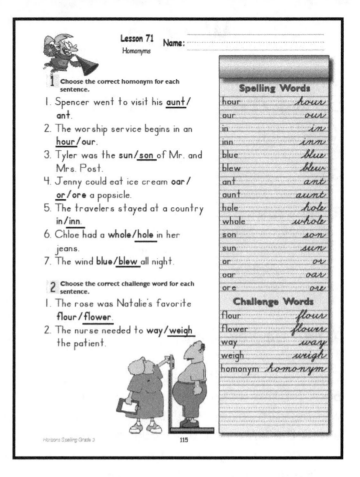

Extended Activities for the Week:

1. Send a list of the week's words home for additional study. You may want to include a letter to the parents urging them to help the students both study and use the words for each week. Emphasize the importance of using spelling words in sentences, in speech, in stories, etc. so that they are given a context and not simply memorized.

2. Challenge students to create lists of additional homonyms. They can look for words they encounter in their other subjects or in their free reading.

3. Have students begin the writing of sentences for each spelling word in their notebooks.

4. Assign the reproducible *Week 15 Worksheet* either as homework or as an added classroom activity.

Lesson 72 – Examine and Explore Words

Teaching Tips:

1. Review homonyms.

2. Have the class read the list of spelling words together with you.

Activities:

1. Give the students the page from the Student Book for this lesson.

2. Review the words in the word box as well as the challenge words.

3. Read the directions with the students. After students have completed the activity sheet, go over the correct answers.

Lesson 72   Name: _____

hour	our	in	inn	blue	blew	ant
aunt	hole	whole	son	sun	or	oar
ore	flour	flower	way	weigh	or	homonyms

1 Fill in the blank with the correct spelling word.
1. Mrs. Richards has a **son** named Brandon.
2. Conner's favorite color is **blue**
3. The train was carrying many tons of iron **ore**
4. The **sun** came out from behind the clouds.
5. The travelers stayed at a country **inn**.
6. The Sunday school program was an **hour** long.
7. The **whole** class went on a field trip.
8. An **ant** is a strong animal for its size.
9. Either Marissa **or** Brittany needed to take the dog for a walk.
10. Jaden's birthday is **in** two days.
11. Weston has a **hole** in his shoe.
12. The strong storm **blew** through the night.
13. **Our** dog is scared of storms.
14. Henry used an **oar** to paddle the kayak.
15. Tom's **aunt** and uncle are coming for a visit.

2 Fill in the blank with the correct challenge word.
1. Mrs. Grove was on her **way** to a business meeting.
2. **Flour** is one of the ingredients in bread.
3. In this lesson you have learned about **homonyms**
4. Mrs. Jefferson planted daisies in her **flower** bed.
5. The butcher needed to **weigh** the meat.

116   Horizons Spelling Grade 3

Extended Activities:

1. Ask students if they can think of other homonyms.

2. Have students continue writing the sentences for each spelling word in their notebooks.

Lesson 73 – Look at Context and Meaning of Words

Teaching Tips:

1. Review words and rules.

2. Give students an opportunity to share any spelling word sentences they have written in their notebooks.

Activities:

1. Give the students the page from the *Student Book* for this lesson.

2. Read the directions on the activity sheet with the students. When they have finished, review the answers as a class.

Extended Activities:

1. Ask students to choose two of the spelling words and draw pictures representing those words. Give an opportunity to share their pictures with the class.

2. Have students continue writing sentences for each spelling word in their notebooks.

3. Give students an opportunity to quiz each other on the spelling words and their definitions.

Lesson 74 - Apply Understanding of Words in Writing

Activities:

1. Give the students the page from the *Student Book* for this lesson.

2. Read the directions for the activity on the sheet.

3. As a class, brainstorm silly sentences that can be made using homonyms.

4. Direct students in sharing their sentences and pictures with the class.

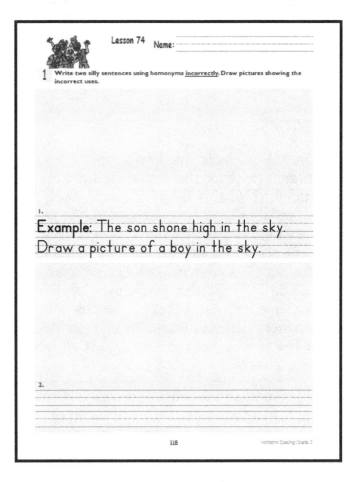

Extended Activities:

1. Have the students continue writing sentences for each spelling word in their notebooks.

Lesson 75 – Assess and Evaluate Progress

Activities:

1. Give the students the page from the *Student Book* for this lesson. Tell the students that this is a "Check-up" page to see what they have learned during the week. (Note: Teachers/parents of home schoolers may decide what will be assessed. If a student does exceptionally well on the "What do you know?" pre-assessment, the teacher may choose not to test words already known by the student. Or the teacher may choose to test all words for the week.)

2. Tell students that you will say a word and use it in a sentence. They will listen to the word and the sentence. Then, they will write the word on the line next to the numbers. All challenge words are included in this review.

3. Say the word. Repeat it in the context of a sentence. Repeat the word.

4. The students write the dictated word.

5. The process is repeated until all words have been tested.

6. The teacher may correct in class by writing the words on the board and having the students compare or "self-correct" their work. The teacher may also correct each student's work individually.

7. The teacher then writes any corrections for words misspelled in the space provided.

8. The students study the misspelled words, and practice them on the second side of the Lesson page.

9. Space is provided for retesting, for testing additional sight or "challenge words" added for the week, and for additional practice.

Check-up time! Lesson 75 Name:

Spelling Test

1. 13.
2. 14.
3. 15.
4. 16.
5. 17.
6. 18.
7. 19.
8. 20.
9. 21.
10. 22.
11. 23.
12. 24.

Corrections

Horizons Spelling Grade 3   119

Extended Activity:

Review any words missed. Send words to review home for additional study. Encourage all students in their efforts.

Week 16 - Skill Review

Lessons 76-80 — Once Again for Excellence

Goal: To review and study the words from Lessons 41-75.

Review rules:
Review the rules for Weeks 9-15.

Teacher's Note:

Students will review 28 words each day from the previous seven weeks. All of the words from the previous weeks will be reviewed. None of the challenge words will be reviewed. Students should know that only 28 words will appear on the final test, which are taken randomly from Weeks 9-15.

What Do You Remember?

Give the students the page from the *Student Book* for this lesson. Tell them that this page will be used to see what they currently know about the review. Ask them to listen carefully to each word as you say it, repeat it in a sentence, and say it once again. Follow the procedures for this page as described in the Introduction at the beginning of this *Teacher's Guide*. Tell students that the challenge words will not be a part of the review.

Week 16 Worksheet Key

Lesson 76 – Practice Makes Perfect

Activities:

1. Give the students the page from the *Student Book* for this lesson.

2. Read to students the directions for the activity sheet. Go over the correct answers as a class.

Extended Activities for the Week:

1. Either send a list of the week's words home for additional study or tell parents that this is a review lesson. You may want to include a letter to the parents urging them to help the students both study and use the words. Emphasize the importance of using spelling words in sentences, in speech, in stories, etc. so that they are given a context and not simply memorized.

2. Assign the reproducible *Week 16 Worksheet* either as homework or as an added classroom activity.

3. You may want to give students spot quizzes to check their spelling of the review words. Emphasize that these quizzes are not graded but are being used to help them review.

Lesson 77 – Revisit for Success

Teaching Tips:

1. Have the class read the list of spelling words together with you.

Activities:

1. Give the students the page from the *Student Book* for this lesson.

2. Review the words in the word box.

3. Read the directions with the students.

4. Ask students to write correctly the words they missed.

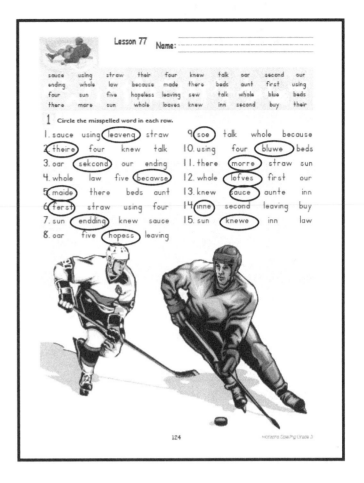

Extended Activities:

1. Ask students to quiz each other on the review words in this lesson.

2. Have students write each spelling word three times using a different color crayon each time.

3. You may want to give students spot quizzes to check their spelling of the review words. Emphasize that these quizzes are not graded but are being used to help them review.

Lesson 78 – Become an Expert

Activities:

1. Give the students the page from the *Student Book* for this lesson.

2. Read the directions on the activity sheet with the students. Have students begin writing the spelling words that mean the same as the written words. Tell students these are called synonyms. Go over the correct responses with the students.

3. Have students complete the middle of the activity sheet. In this section they will write antonyms or words that mean the opposite of the given word. Go over those answers as well.

4. Have students finish by writing the words that were not used.

Extended Activities:

1. Ask students to choose two of the spelling words and draw pictures representing those words. Give an opportunity to share their pictures with the class.

2. Have students continue the writing of sentences sentences for each spelling word in their notebooks.

3. You may want to give students spot quizzes to check their spelling of the review words. Emphasize that these quizzes are not graded but are being used to help them review.

Lesson 79 – Exercise for Mastery

Activities:

1. Give the students the page from the *Student Book* for this lesson.

2. Read the directions on the sheet.

3. As a class, brainstorm things that students see in the playground picture. Maybe point out some different ways of looking at the picture that will incorporate the spelling words.

4. Direct students in completing the activity sheet.

Extended Activities:

1. Share stories.

2. Extend the activity by having students write about other things they might see on a playground. They should again work to include their spelling words.

3. You may want to give students spot quizzes to check their spelling of the review words. Emphasize that these quizzes are not graded but are being used to help them review.

Lesson 80 – Assess and Evaluate

Activities:

1. Give the students the page from the *Student Book* for this lesson. Tell the students that this is a "Check-up" page to see what they have learned over the past seven weeks.

2. Tell students that you will say a word and use it in a sentence. They will listen to the word and the sentence. Then, they will write the word on the line next to the numbers.

3. Say the word. Repeat it in the context of a sentence. Repeat the word.

4. The students write the dictated word.

5. The process is repeated until all words have been tested.

6. The teacher may correct in class by writing the words on the board and having the students compare or "self-correct" their work. The teacher may also correct each student's work individually.

7. The teacher then writes any corrections for words misspelled in the space provided.

8. The students study the misspelled words, and practice them on the second side of the Lesson page.

Final Test:

falling	seven	wash
son	holding	ending
talk	hunting	dresses
by	naughty	ten
eight	six	loves
tall	pear	showing
fourth	paws	aunt
tries	jumping	three
came	more	blue
water		

Extended Activity:

Review any words missed. Encourage all students in their efforts.

Week 17

Lessons 81-85 — Assess Student's Knowledge

Goal: To review and study words with silent letters *mb, kn, wr, qu,* and *ck.*

Review rules:

The consonant diagraph *mb* stands for the *m* sound.

The consonant diagraph *kn* stands for the *n* sound.

The consonant diagraph *wr* stands for the *r* sound.

The consonant diagraph *qu* stands for the *kw* sound. The letter *u* is a silent partner and is not a sounded vowel.

The consonant diagraph *ck* stands for the *k* sound.

What Do You Know?

Give the students the page from the *Student Book* for this lesson. Tell them that this page will be used to see what they currently know about the words for the week. Ask them to listen carefully to each word as you say it, repeat it in a sentence, and say it once again. Follow the procedures for this page as described in the Introduction at the beginning of this *Teacher's Guide*.

Show students how to write their assigned Challenge Words in the appropriate section at the back of their *Spelling Dictionary*.

What do you know? Lessons 81-85   Name: _____

Words for the Week

1. comb
2. knife
3. knee
4. write
5. wrong
6. wrap
7. black
8. crack
9. duck
10. climb
11. lamb
12. thumb
13. quick
14. squeal
15. quiet
16. tackle
17. chicken
18. knowledge
19. crackers
20. honeycomb

Practice

Horizons Spelling Grade 3   129

Week 17 Worksheet Key

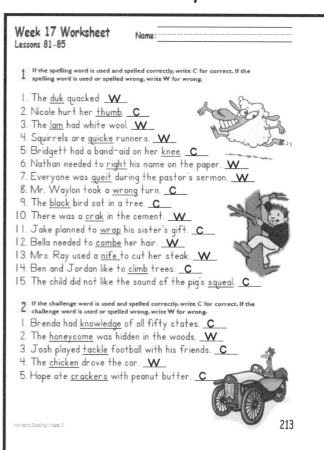

Week 17 Worksheet   Name: _____
Lessons 81-85

1 If the spelling word is used and spelled correctly, write C for correct. If the spelling word is used or spelled wrong, write W for wrong.

1. The <u>duk</u> quacked. **W**
2. Nicole hurt her <u>thumb</u>. **C**
3. The <u>lam</u> had white wool. **W**
4. Squirrels are <u>quicke</u> runners. **W**
5. Bridgett had a band-aid on her <u>knee</u>. **C**
6. Nathan needed to <u>right</u> his name on the paper. **W**
7. Everyone was <u>queit</u> during the pastor's sermon. **W**
8. Mr. Waylon took a <u>wrong</u> turn. **C**
9. The <u>black</u> bird sat in a tree. **C**
10. There was a <u>crak</u> in the cement. **W**
11. Jake planned to <u>wrap</u> his sister's gift. **C**
12. Bella needed to <u>combe</u> her hair. **W**
13. Mrs. Ray used a <u>nife</u> to cut her steak. **W**
14. Ben and Jordan like to <u>climb</u> trees. **C**
15. The child did not like the sound of the pig's <u>squeal</u>. **C**

2 If the challenge word is used and spelled correctly, write C for correct. If the challenge word is used or spelled wrong, write W for wrong.

1. Brenda had <u>knowledge</u> of all fifty states. **C**
2. The <u>honeycome</u> was hidden in the woods. **W**
3. Josh played <u>tackle</u> football with his friends. **C**
4. The <u>chicken</u> drove the car. **W**
5. Hope ate <u>crackers</u> with peanut butter. **C**

Horizons Spelling Grade 3   213

Lesson 81 – Introduce Words

Activities:

1. Give the students the page from the *Student Book* for this lesson.

2. Read to students the directions for the activity on the sheet.

3. Go over the answers after students have completed the activity sheet.

4. Instruct students to write their assigned Challenge Words in their *Spelling Dictionaries* in the back section. Words are to be written under the correct letter of the alphabet.

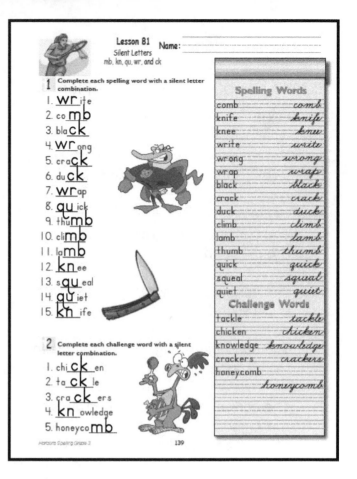

Extended Activities for the Week:

1. Send a list of the week's words home for additional study. You may want to include a letter to the parents urging them to help the students both study and use the words for each week. Emphasize the importance of using spelling words in sentences, in speech, in stories, etc. so that they are given a context and not simply memorized.

2. Challenge students to create lists of additional words with *mb, kn, wr*, and *ck*. They can look for words they encounter in their other subjects or in their free reading. Maybe some of the students' names have these letter combinations.

3. Have students begin the writing of sentences for each spelling word in their notebooks.

4. Assign the reproducible *Week 17 Worksheet* either as homework or as an added classroom activity.

Lesson 82 – Examine and Explore Words

Teaching Tips:

1. Review the letter combinations *mb, kn, wr, qu,* and *ck* students are working with for the week.

2. Have the class read the list of spelling words together with you.

Activities:

1. Give the students the page from the *Student Book* for this lesson.

2. Review the words in the word box as well as the challenge words.

3. Read the directions with the students. Direct them in putting the words under the correct categories.

4. Have students complete the word challenge section of the activity sheet.

Extended Activities:

1. Write your words as if they are a part of a ransom note. Cut out letters in a newspaper or magazine to spell the words. Glue the words on a piece of paper.

2. Have students continue writing the sentences for each spelling word in their notebooks.

Lesson 83 - Look at Context and Meaning of Words

Teaching Tips:

1. Review words and rules.

2. Give students an opportunity to share any spelling word sentences they have written in their notebooks.

Activities:

1. Give the students the page from the *Student Book* for this lesson.

2. Read the directions on the activity sheet with the students. When they have finished, review the answers as a class.

3. Have students complete the challenge word section of the activity sheet. Go over those answers as well.

Lesson 83   Name: _____

comb   knife   knee   write   wrong   wrap   black
crack   duck   climb   lamb   thumb   quick   squeal
quiet   tackle   chicken   knowledge   crackers   honeycomb

1 Fill in the blank with the correct spelling word.

1. The __lamb__ followed the other sheep into the barn.
2. Mrs. Owens made a __quick__ trip to the grocery store.
3. The infant likes to suck her __thumb__.
4. The sidewalk had a large __crack__.
5. Mrs. Atkins told her son to __comb__ his hair.
6. There was a large __duck__ in the pond.
7. Mr. Reeve took a __wrong__ turn in the unfamiliar city.
8. Cole used a __knife__ to butter his bread.
9. The men planned to __climb__ to the top of the mountain.
10. Grace scraped her __knee__ on the rock.
11. Mrs. Harper planned to __wrap__ her Christmas presents on Saturday.
12. Gavin needed a new pair of __black__ shoes.
13. Each student was asked to __write__ a sentence.
14. The teacher asked her students to be __quiet__.
15. Paxton did not like the __squeal__ the pig made.

2 Fill in the blank with the correct challenge word.

1. The bee keeper removed the __honeycomb__.
2. Cole liked to put __crackers__ in his soup.
3. Sophie studied hard to get more __knowledge__.
4. The football players tried to __tackle__ the runner.
5. The __chicken__ escaped from the pen.

Horizons Spelling Grade 3   133

Extended Activities:

1. Use your computer to type your spelling words. Use different fonts to make them more interesting.

2. Have students continue writing sentences for each spelling word in their notebooks.

3. Give students an opportunity to quiz each other on the spelling words and their definitions.

Lesson 84 – Apply Understanding of Words in Writing

Activities:

1. Give the students the page from the *Student Book* for this lesson.

2. Read the directions for the activity.

3. As a class, brainstorm scenes that a person might see at a farm.

4. Direct students in drawing their pictures and writing their sentences.

Lesson 84   Name: _____

comb	knife	knee	write	wrong
wrap	black	crack	duck	climb
lamb	thumb	quick	squeal	quiet

1 Draw a picture of a farm scene. Use four of your spelling words to write about the picture you drew.

Example: At the farm I saw a lamb and a duck. I heard a pig squeal. I also saw a black and white cow.

134   Horizons Spelling Grade 3

Extended Activities:

1. Share sentences.

2. Share pictures.

3. Have the students continue writing sentences for each spelling word in their notebooks.

Lesson 85 – Assess and Evaluate Progress

Activities:

1. Give the students the page from the *Student Book* for this lesson. Tell the students that this is a "Check-up" page to see what they have learned during the week. (Note: Teachers/parents of home schoolers may decide what will be assessed. If a student does exceptionally well on the "What do you know?" pre-assessment, the teacher may choose not to test words already known by the student. Or the teacher may choose to test all words for the week.)

2. Tell students that you will say a word and use it in a sentence. They will listen to the word and the sentence. Then, they will write the word on the line next to the numbers. All challenge words are included in this review.

3. Say the word. Repeat it in the context of a sentence. Repeat the word.

4. The students write the dictated word.

5. The process is repeated until all words have been tested.

6. The teacher may correct in class by writing the words on the board and having the students compare or "self-correct" their work. The teacher may also correct each student's work individually.

7. The teacher then writes any corrections for words misspelled in the space provided.

8. The students study the misspelled words, and practice them on the second side of the Lesson page.

9. Space is provided for retesting, for testing additional sight or "challenge words" added for the week, and for additional practice.

Check-up time!   Lesson 85   Name:

Spelling Test

1. _____   13. _____
2. _____   14. _____
3. _____   15. _____
4. _____   16. _____
5. _____   17. _____
6. _____   18. _____
7. _____   19. _____
8. _____   20. _____
9. _____   21. _____
10. _____   22. _____
11. _____   23. _____
12. _____   24. _____

Corrections

Horizons Spelling Grade 3   135

Extended Activity:

Review any words missed. Send words to review home for additional study. Encourage all students in their efforts.

Week 18

Lessons 86-90 — Assess Student's Knowledge

Goal: To review and study words with the *ou* and *oi* sounds.

Review rules:

The *ou* sound can be spelled *ou* or *ow* as in the words house and how.

The *oi* sound can be spelled *oi* or *oy* as in the words point and enjoy.

What Do You Know?

Give the students the page from the *Student Book* for this lesson. Tell them that this page will be used to see what they currently know about the words for the week. Ask them to listen carefully to each word as you say it, repeat it in a sentence, and say it once again. Follow the procedures for this page as described in the Introduction at the beginning of this *Teacher's Guide*.

Show students how to write their assigned Challenge Words in the appropriate section at the back of their *Spelling Dictionary*.

Week 18 Worksheet Key

Lesson 86 – Introduce Words

Activities:

1. Give the students the page from the *Student Book* for this lesson.

2. Read to students the directions for the first activity on the sheet.

3. Direct students in completing the second part of the activity sheet.

4. Instruct students to write their assigned Challenge Words in their *Spelling Dictionaries* in the back section. Words are to be written under the correct letter of the alphabet.

Extended Activities for the Week:

1. Send a list of the week's words home for additional study. You may want to include a letter to the parents urging them to help the students both study and use the words for each week. Emphasize the importance of using spelling words in sentences, in speech, in stories, etc. so that they are given a context and not simply memorized.

2. Challenge students to create lists of additional words with the *ou* or *oi* sounds. They can look for words they encounter in their other subjects or in their free reading. Maybe some of the students' names have *ou* or *oi* sounds.

3. Have students begin the writing of sentences for each spelling word in their notebooks.

4. Assign the reproducible *Week 18 Worksheet* either as homework or as an added classroom activity.

Lesson 87 - Examine and Explore Words

Teaching Tips:

1. Review the words students are working with for the week.

2. Have the class read the list of spelling words together with you.

Activities:

1. Give the students the page from the *Student Book* for this lesson.

2. Review the words in the word box as well as the challenge words.

3. Read the directions with the students. Go over the correct responses when students have finished.

4. Have students complete the challenge word section of the activity sheet.

Extended Activities:

1. Ask students if they can think of other words that have the *ou* or *oi* sounds highlighted in the spelling words of the week.

2. Have students continue writing the sentences for each spelling word in their notebooks.

Lesson 88 – Look at Context and Meaning of Words

Teaching Tips:

1. Review words and rules.

2. Give students an opportunity to share any spelling word sentences they have written in their notebooks.

Activities:

1. Give the students the page from the *Student Book* for this lesson.

2. Read the directions on the activity sheet with the students. When they have finished, review the answers as a class.

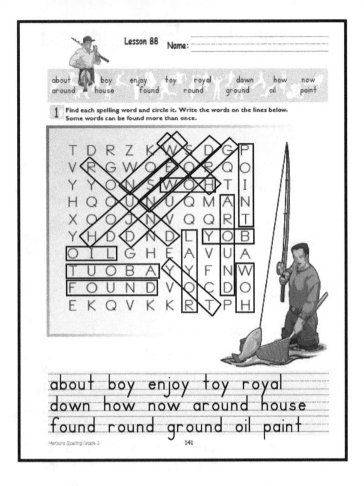

Extended Activities:

1. Have students write each of their spelling words forward and backward.

2. Ask students to choose two of the spelling words and draw pictures representing those words. Give an opportunity to share their pictures with the class.

3. Have students continue writing sentences for each spelling word in their notebooks.

4. Give students an opportunity to quiz each other on the spelling words and their definitions.

Lesson 89 – Apply Understanding of Words in Writing

Activities:

1. Give the students the page from the *Student Book* for this lesson.

2. Read the directions for the activity on the sheet.

3. As a class, brainstorm possible sentences that can be made from the spelling words. You may want to use one of the provided examples.

4. Direct students in completing the activity sheet and drawing pictures.

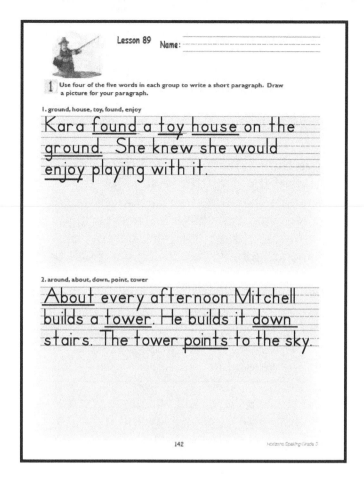

Extended Activities:

1. Share stories.

2. Share pictures.

3. Have the students continue writing sentences for each spelling word in their notebooks.

Lesson 90 – Assess and Evaluate Progress

Activities:

1. Give the students the page from the *Student Book* for this lesson. Tell the students that this is a "Check-up" page to see what they have learned during the week. (Note: Teachers/parents of home schoolers may decide what will be assessed. If a student does exceptionally well on the "What do you know?" pre-assessment, the teacher may choose not to test words already known by the student. Or the teacher may choose to test all words for the week.)

2. Tell students that you will say a word and use it in a sentence. They will listen to the word and the sentence. Then, they will write the word on the line next to the numbers. All challenge words are included in this review.

3. Say the word. Repeat it in the context of a sentence. Repeat the word.

4. The students write the dictated word.

5. The process is repeated until all words have been tested.

6. The teacher may correct in class by writing the words on the board and having the students compare or "self-correct" their work. The teacher may also correct each student's work individually.

7. The teacher then writes any corrections for words misspelled in the space provided.

8. The students study the misspelled words, and practice them on the second side of the Lesson page.

9. Space is provided for retesting, for testing additional sight or "challenge words" added for the week, and for additional practice.

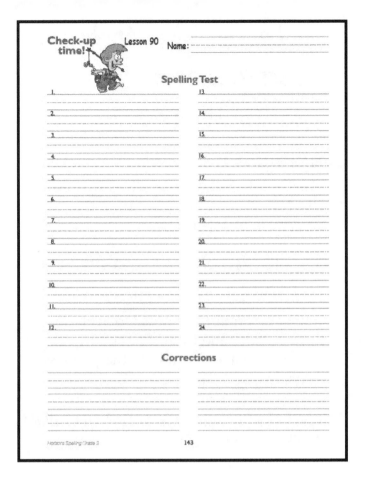

Extended Activity:

Review any words missed. Send words to review home for additional study. Encourage all students in their efforts.

Week 19

Lessons 91-95 — Assess Student's Knowledge

Goal: To review and study words with the *s* and *j* sounds.

Review rules:

The *s* sound can be spelled *s*, *c*, or *ss* as in the words sin, center, and press.

The *j* sound can be spelled: *g* or *j* as in page and jump.

What Do You Know?

Give the students the page from the *Student Book* for this lesson. Tell them that this page will be used to see what they currently know about the words for the week. Ask them to listen carefully to each word as you say it, repeat it in a sentence, and say it once again. Follow the procedures for this page as described in the Introduction at the beginning of this *Teacher's Guide*.

Show students how to write their assigned challenge words in the appropriate section at the back of their *Spelling Dictionary*.

Week 19 Worksheet Key

Lesson 91 – Introduce Words

Activities:

1. Give the students the page from the *Student Book* for this lesson.

2. Read to students the directions for the activity on the sheet. Have them put the spelling words in the correct categories.

3. Instruct students to write their assigned challenge words in their *Spelling Dictionaries* in the back section. Words are to be written under the correct letter of the alphabet.

Extended Activities for the Week:

1. Send a list of the week's words home for additional study. You may want to include a letter to the parents urging them to help the students both study and use the words for each week. Emphasize the importance of using spelling words in sentences, in speech, in stories, etc. so that they are given a context and not simply memorized.

2. Challenge students to create lists of additional words with the *s* and *j* sounds. They can look for words they encounter in their other subjects or in their free reading. Maybe some of the students' names have *s* or *j* sounds.

3. Have students begin the writing of sentences for each spelling word in their notebooks.

4. Assign the reproducible *Week 19 Worksheet* either as homework or as an added classroom activity.

Horizons Spelling Grade 3

Lesson 92 – Examine and Explore Words

Teaching Tips:

1. Review the spelling words with *s* and *j* sounds students are working with for the week.

2. Have the class read the list of spelling words together with you.

Activities:

1. Give the students the page from the *Student Book* for this lesson.

2. Review the words in the word box as well as the challenge words.

3. Read the directions with the students. They will be asked to fill in the blanks with the correct spelling words.

4. Go over the correct answers with the class.

Extended Activities:

1. Ask students if they can think of other words that have the *s* or *j* sounds highlighted in the spelling words of the week.

2. Students could write each spelling word forward and backward.

3. Have students continue writing the sentences for each spelling word in their notebooks.

Lesson 93 – Look at Context and Meaning of Words

Teaching Tips:

1. Review words and rules.

2. Give students an opportunity to share any spelling word sentences they have written in their notebooks.

Activities:

1. Give the students the page from the *Student Book* for this lesson.

2. Read the directions on the activity sheet with the students. Review the definitions of synonyms and antonyms.

3. When they have finished, review the answers as a class.

Extended Activities:

1. Have students write their spelling words in chalk on the sidewalk. When they are finished, you can clean the sidewalk with water.

2. Ask students to choose two of the spelling words and draw pictures representing those words. Give an opportunity to share their pictures with the class.

3. Have students continue writing sentences for each spelling word in their notebooks.

4. Give students an opportunity to quiz each other on the spelling words and their definitions.

Lesson 94 – Apply Understanding of Words in Writing

Activities:

1. Give the students the page from the *Student Book* for this lesson.

2. Read the directions for the activity sheet.

3. As a class, brainstorm ways a person might describe how Jesus has saved him or her from their sins.

4. Direct students in completing the activities.

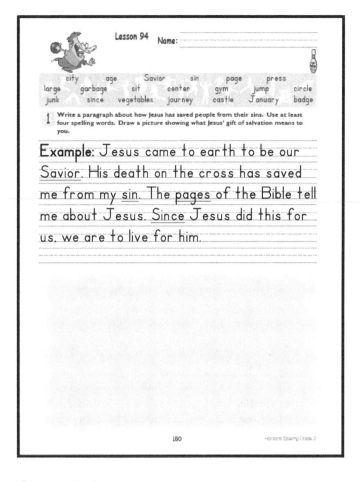

Extended Activities:

1. Share paragraphs.

2. Share pictures.

3. Have the students continue writing sentences for each spelling word in their notebooks.

Lesson 95 – Assess and Evaluate Progress

Activities:

1. Give the students the page from the *Student Book* for this lesson. Tell the students that this is a "Check-up" page to see what they have learned during the week. (Note: Teachers/parents of home schoolers may decide what will be assessed. If a student does exceptionally well on the "What do you know?" pre-assessment, the teacher may choose not to test words already known by the student. Or the teacher may choose to test all words for the week.)

2. Tell students that you will say a word and use it in a sentence. They will listen to the word and the sentence. Then, they will write the word on the line next to the numbers. All challenge words are included in this review.

3. Say the word. Repeat it in the context of a sentence. Repeat the word.

4. The students write the dictated word.

5. The process is repeated until all words have been tested.

6. The teacher may correct in class by writing the words on the board and having the students compare or "self-correct" their work. The teacher may also correct each student's work individually.

7. The teacher then writes any corrections for words misspelled in the space provided.

8. The students study the misspelled words, and practice them on the second side of the Lesson page.

9. Space is provided for retesting, for testing additional sight or "challenge words" added for the week, and for additional practice.

Check-up time!   Lesson 95   Name: _____

Spelling Test

1. _____   13. _____
2. _____   14. _____
3. _____   15. _____
4. _____   16. _____
5. _____   17. _____
6. _____   18. _____
7. _____   19. _____
8. _____   20. _____
9. _____   21. _____
10. _____   22. _____
11. _____   23. _____
12. _____   24. _____

Corrections

Horizons Spelling Grade 3   161

Extended Activity:

Review any words missed. Send words to review home for additional study. Encourage all students in their efforts.

Week 20

Lessons 96-100 — Assess Student's Knowledge

Goal: To review and study words with the double *ee* and *oo*.

Review rules:

The sound of the *ee* is *ē* as in the words *keep* and *bee*.

The sound of the *oo* is *ŏŏ* as in the words *school* and *soon*.

What Do You Know?

Give the students the page from the *Student Book* for this lesson. Tell them that this page will be used to see what they currently know about the words for the week. Ask them to listen carefully to each word as you say it, repeat it in a sentence, and say it once again. Follow the procedures for this page as described in the Introduction at the beginning of this *Teacher's Guide*.

Show students how to write their assigned challenge words in the appropriate section at the back of their *Spelling Dictionary*.

Week 20 Worksheet Key

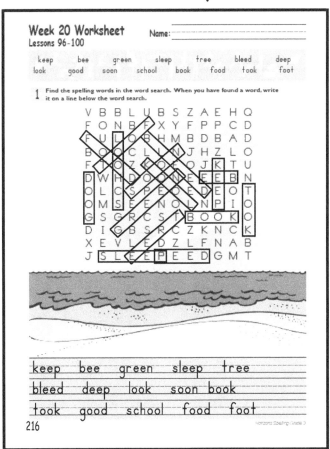

Lesson 96 – Introduce Words

Activities:

1. Give the students the page from the *Student Book* for this lesson.

2. Read to students the directions for the first activity on the sheet.

3. Direct students in completing the second part of the activity sheet.

4. Instruct students to write their assigned challenge words in their *Spelling Dictionaries* in the back section. Words are to be written under the correct letter of the alphabet.

Extended Activities for the Week:

1. Send a list of the week's words home for additional study. You may want to include a letter to the parents urging them to help the students both study and use the words for each week. Emphasize the importance of using spelling words in sentences, in speech, in stories, etc. so that they are given a context and not simply memorized.

2. Challenge students to create lists of additional words with double *e*'s or *o*'s. They can look for words they encounter in their other subjects or in their free reading. Maybe some of the students' names have double *e*'s or *o*'s.

3. Have students begin the writing of sentences for each spelling word in their notebooks.

4. Assign the reproducible *Week 20 Worksheet* either as homework or as an added classroom activity.

118

Lesson 97 – Examine and Explore Words

Teaching Tips:

1. Review the *ee* and *oo* words students are working with for the week.

2. Have the class read the list of spelling words together with you.

Activities:

1. Give the students the page from the *Student Book* for this lesson.

2. Review the words in the word box as well as the challenge words.

3. Read the directions with the students. Emphasize that not all of the spelling words will be used in the crossword puzzle.

4. Go over the correct answers with the class.

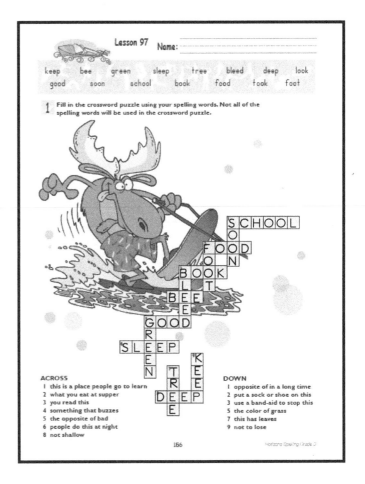

Extended Activities:

1. Ask students if they can think of other words that have *ee* or *oo* highlighted in the spelling words of the week.

2. Have students continue writing the sentences for each spelling word in their notebooks.

3. Ask students to look at pages in a newspaper and see how many of their spelling words they can find. You may want to break students in pairs and give each pair one page of the newspaper.

Lesson 98 – Look at Context and Meaning of Words

Teaching Tips:

1. Review words and rules.

2. Give students an opportunity to share any spelling word sentences they have written in their notebooks.

Activities:

1. Give the students the page from the *Student Book* for this lesson.

2. Read the directions on the activity sheet with the students. When they have finished, review the answers as a class.

3. Have students complete the challenge words portion of the activity sheet. Go over those answers as well.

Extended Activities:

1. Use scrabble tiles to write your spelling words.

2. Ask students to choose two of the spelling words and draw pictures representing those words. Give an opportunity to share their pictures with the class.

3. Have students continue writing sentences for each spelling word in their notebooks.

4. Give students an opportunity to quiz each other on the spelling words and their definitions.

Lesson 98 Name: _____

keep   bee   green   sleep   tree   bleed   deep
look   good   soon   school   book   food   took
foot   cheese   cookie   shook   creep   goose

1 Fill in the blank with the correct spelling word.
1. Carter made sure to **look** both ways before crossing the street.
2. The **school** had a red door.
3. Jesse was a **good** student.
4. Casey didn't like to swim in the **deep** end.
5. Bailey checked out a **book** from the library.
6. The **tree** was taller than the house.
7. Kayla put a band-aid on the cut so it would not **bleed** on her clothes.
8. Mrs. Crane put the **food** on the table.
9. The tree had **green** leaves.
10. The family would leave on vacation **soon**.
11. The baby went to **sleep** after lunch.
12. The **bee** landed on the flower.
13. The brick was one **foot** long.
14. Nick **took** the bus to school.
15. Miriam likes to **keep** her door open at night.

2 Fill in the blank with the correct challenge word.
1. Mrs. Blain put a piece of **cheese** on the bread.
2. The thunder **shook** the house.
3. The **goose** lived in the barn.
4. Jon ate a chocolate chip **cookie**.
5. The baby learned to **creep**.

Lesson 99 – Apply Understanding of Words in Writing

Activities:

1. Give the students the page from the *Student Book* for this lesson.

2. Read the directions for the activity on the sheet.

3. As a class, discuss the picture. Think of different scenes that could be played out in the meadow.

4. Direct students in writing a description of the picture using five of their spelling words.

Extended Activities:

1. Share descriptions.

2. Ask students to write each of the spelling words on a piece of paper. Ask students to trace around each word three times using a different colored pencil each time. As they trace, they should silently think of each letter of the word.

3. Have the students continue writing sentences for each spelling word in their notebooks.

Lesson 100 – Assess and Evaluate Progress

Activities:

1. Give the students the page from the *Student Book* for this lesson. Tell the students that this is a "Check-up" page to see what they have learned during the week. (Note: Teachers/parents of home schoolers may decide what will be assessed. If a student does exceptionally well on the "What do you know?" pre-assessment, the teacher may choose not to test words already known by the student. Or the teacher may choose to test all words for the week.

2. Tell students that you will say a word and use it in a sentence. They will listen to the word and the sentence. Then, they will write the word on the line next to the numbers. All challenge words are included in this review.

3. Say the word. Repeat it in the context of a sentence. Repeat the word.

4. The students write the dictated word.

5. The process is repeated until all words have been tested.

6. The teacher may correct in class by writing the words on the board and having the students compare or "self-correct" their work. The teacher may also correct each student's work individually.

7. The teacher then writes any corrections for words misspelled in the space provided.

8. The students study the misspelled words, and practice them on the second side of the Lesson page.

9. Space is provided for retesting, for testing additional sight or "challenge words" added for the week, and for additional practice.

Extended Activity:

Review any words missed. Send words to review home for additional study. Encourage all students in their efforts.

122

Week 21

Lessons 101-105 — Assess Student's Knowledge

Goal: To review and study the *gh* letter combination.

Review rules:

The letter combination *gh* can be silent in words such as *light* and *through*.

The letter combination *gh* can make the *f* sound in words such as *tough* and *laugh*.

The letter combination *gh* can make the *g* sound in words such as *ghost* and *ghetto*.

What Do You Know?

Give the students the page from the *Student Book* for this lesson. Tell them that this page will be used to see what they currently know about the words for the week. Ask them to listen carefully to each word as you say it, repeat it in a sentence, and say it once again. Follow the procedures for this page as described in the Introduction at the beginning of this *Teacher's Guide*.

Show students how to write their assigned challenge words in the appropriate section at the back of their *Spelling Dictionary*.

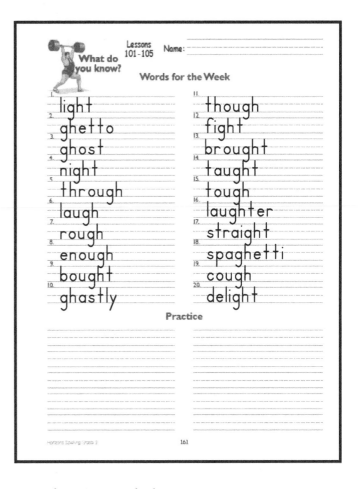

Week 21 Worksheet Key

Lesson 101 – Introduce Words

Activities:

1. Give the students the page from the *Student Book* for this lesson.

2. Read to students the directions for the activity sheet. Go over the correct answers.

3. Direct students in completing the challenge word part of the activity sheet.

4. Instruct students to write their assigned challenge words in their *Spelling Dictionaries* in the back section. Words are to be written under the correct letter of the alphabet.

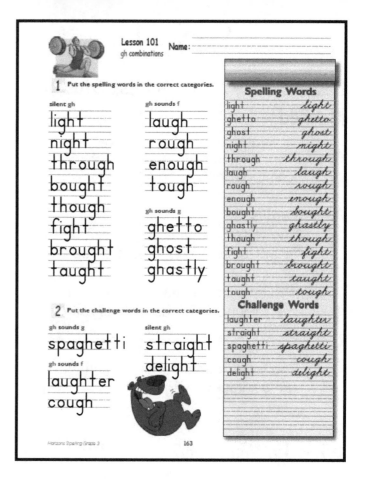

Extended Activities for the Week:

1. Send a list of the week's words home for additional study. You may want to include a letter to the parents urging them to help the students both study and use the words for each week. Emphasize the importance of using spelling words in sentences, in speech, in stories, etc. so that they are given a context and not simply memorized.

2. Challenge students to create lists of additional words with the *gh* combination sounded *f*, *g* and silent. They can look for words they encounter in their other subjects or in their free reading.

3. Have students begin the writing of sentences for each spelling word in their notebooks.

4. Assign the reproducible *Week 21 Worksheet* either as homework or as an added classroom activity.

Lesson 102 – Examine and Explore Words

Teaching Tips:

1. Review the *gh* letter combinations students are working with for the week.

2. Have the class read the list of spelling words together with you.

Activities:

1. Give the students the page from the *Student Book* for this lesson.

2. Read the directions with the students. After they have completed the activity, go over the correct responses together as a class.

3. Have students complete the challenge word section of the activity sheet as well.

Extended Activities:

1. Have students design a bookmark with all of their spelling words.

2. Ask students if they can think of other words that have *gh* highlighted in the spelling words of the week.

3. Have students continue writing the sentences for each spelling word in their notebooks.

Lesson 103 – Look at Context and Meaning of Words

Teaching Tips:

1. Review words and rules.

2. Give students an opportunity to share any spelling word sentences they have written in their notebooks.

Activities:

1. Give the students the page from the *Student Book* for this lesson.

2. Read the directions on the activity sheet with the students. When they have finished, review the answers as a class.

3. Have students complete the challenge word portion of the activity sheet. Go over those answers as well.

Lesson 103   Name: _____

light   ghetto   ghost   night   through   laugh   rough
enough   bought   ghastly   though   fight   brought   taught
tough   laughter   straight   spaghetti   cough   delight

1 Fill in the blank with the spelling word that best completes each sentence.
1. The third graders found it **tough** to climb the rope.
2. A cat has a **rough** tongue.
3. Mr. Granger **taught** fifth grade.
4. There was **enough** ice cream for everyone.
5. Jenny **bought** a new toothbrush.
6. The story had a **ghost** as a main character.
7. "Silent **Night**" is the name of a Christmas song.
8. The rabbit jumped **through** the hedge.
9. Tony **brought** chips to the party.
10. The **ghetto** needed new street lights.
11. The clown made the children **laugh**.
12. Beau put on the kitchen **light**.
13. The puppies **fight** over a bowl of food.
14. The patient had a **ghastly** cut.
15. Laura played outside even **though** it was raining.

2 Fill in the blank with the challenge word that best completes each sentence.
1. Mrs. Davidson made a **spaghetti** supper.
2. A ruler has a **straight** edge.
3. Clay had a **cough** and a cold.
4. The sound of **laughter** was heard from the playground.
5. Bella took **delight** in her new puppy.

Horizons Spelling Grade 3   165

Extended Activities:

1. Have students use alphabet cereal to write their spelling words.

2. Ask students to choose two of the spelling words and draw pictures representing those words. Give an opportunity to share their pictures with the class.

3. Have students continue writing sentences for each spelling word in their notebooks.

4. Give students an opportunity to quiz each other on the spelling words and their definitions.

Lesson 104 – Apply Understanding of Words in Writing

Activities:

1. Give the students the page from the *Student Book* for this lesson.

2. Read the directions for activity on the sheet.

3. When the students have finished, call on several students to read the sentences that they have written.

4. As an added activity, have students draw pictures of images that come to mind after reading these spelling words.

Extended Activities:

1. Have students think of songs that contain their spelling words.

2. Share pictures.

3. Have the students continue writing sentences for each spelling word in their notebooks.

Lesson 105 – Assess and Evaluate Progress

Activities:

1. Give the students the page from the *Student Book* for this lesson. Tell the students that this is a "Check-up" page to see what they have learned during the week. (Note: Teachers/parents of home schoolers may decide what will be assessed. If a student does exceptionally well on the "What do you know?" pre-assessment, the teacher may choose not to test words already known by the student. Or the teacher may choose to test all words for the week.)

2. Tell students that you will say a word and use it in a sentence. They will listen to the word and the sentence. Then, they will write the word on the line next to the numbers. All challenge words are included in this review.

3. Say the word. Repeat it in the context of a sentence. Repeat the word.

4. The students write the dictated word.

5. The process is repeated until all words have been tested.

6. The teacher may correct in class by writing the words on the board and having the students compare or "self-correct" their work. The teacher may also correct each student's work individually.

7. The teacher then writes any corrections for words misspelled in the space provided.

8. The students study the misspelled words, and practice them on the second side of the Lesson page.

9. Space is provided for retesting, for testing additional sight or "challenge words" added for the week, and for additional practice.

Extended Activity:

Review any words missed. Send words to review home for additional study. Encourage all students in their efforts.

Week 22

Lessons 106-110 — Assess Student's Knowledge

Goal: To review and study irregular verb tenses.

Review rules:

Regular verbs add *ed* when changing from present to past and past participle.

Not all verbs follow the regular pattern when changing from present to past and past participle.

What Do You Know?

Give the students the page from the *Student Book* for this lesson. Tell them that this page will be used to see what they currently know about the words for the week. Ask them to listen carefully to each word as you say it, repeat it in a sentence, and say it once again. Follow the procedures for this page as described in the Introduction at the beginning of this

Show students how to write their assigned challenge words in the appropriate section at the back of their *Spelling Dictionary*.

Week 22 Worksheet Key

Lesson 106 – Introduce Words

Activities:

1. Give the students the page from the *Student Book* for this lesson.

2. Read to students the directions for the first activity on the sheet. Go over the correct answers as a class.

3. Direct students in completing the challenge word section of the activity sheet.

4. Instruct students to write their assigned challenge words in their *Spelling Dictionaries* in the back section. Words are to be written under the correct letter of the alphabet.

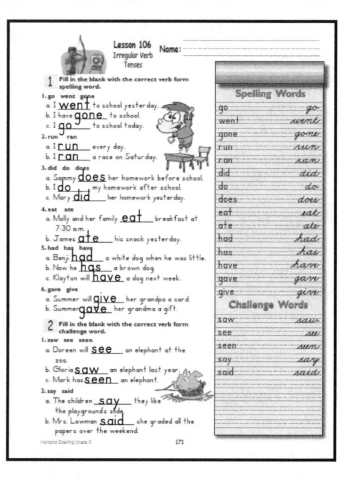

Extended Activities for the Week:

1. Send a list of the week's words home for additional study. You may want to include a letter to the parents urging them to help the students both study and use the words for each week. Emphasize the importance of using spelling words in sentences, in speech, in stories, etc. so that they are given a context and not simply memorized.

2. Challenge students to create lists of additional irregular verbs. They can look for words they encounter in their other subjects or in their free reading.

3. Have students begin the writing of sentences for each spelling word in their notebooks.

4. Assign the reproducible *Week 22 Worksheet* either as homework or as an added classroom activity.

Lesson 107 – Examine and Explore Words

Teaching Tips:

1. Review the irregular verbs students are working with for the week.

2. Have the class read the list of spelling words together with you.

Activities:

1. Give the students the page from the *Student Book* for this lesson.

2. Review the words on both sides of the matching activity.

3. Read the directions with the students. Remind them that some of the words will be matched more than once.

4. Go over the correct answers with the class.

Extended Activities:

1. Ask students if they can think of other words that are irregular verbs highlighted in the spelling words of the week.

2. Have students continue writing the sentences for each spelling word in their notebooks.

Lesson 108 – Look at Context and Meaning of Words

Teaching Tips:

1. Review words and rules.

2. Give students an opportunity to share any spelling word sentences they have written in their notebooks.

Activities:

1. Give the students the page from the *Student Book* for this lesson.

2. Read the directions on the activity sheet with the students. When they have finished, review the answers as a class.

3. Have students complete the challenge word section of the activity sheet. Go over those answers as well.

Lesson 108   Name: _____

1 Indicate if the spelling word is used correctly or not. C – correct W – wrong
1. Stephan <u>went</u> to Tulsa for Christmas. **C**
2. Lauren <u>do</u> not know the problem's answers. **W**
3. Miranda <u>give</u> her lunch to Sara. **W**
4. Elise <u>eat</u> ice cream for dessert. **W**
5. Kurt <u>had</u> a cut on his elbow last week. **C**
6. Anna <u>have</u> a new bike. **W**
7. Heidi <u>gave</u> her mom a dandelion. **C**
8. Jill liked to <u>run</u> in her new shoes. **C**
9. All of the ice cream was <u>gone</u>. **C**
10. Cassidy <u>did</u> eat her hamburger tomorrow. **W**
11. Seth <u>ate</u> an apple yesterday. **C**
12. <u>Does</u> your mother know how to knit? **C**
13. Mr. Green <u>ran</u> a mile. **C**
14. Ross <u>go</u> to the doctor last week. **W**
15. Max and Karina <u>has</u> a baby brother. **W**

2 Indicate if the challenge word is used correctly or not. C – correct W – wrong
1. I <u>saw</u> an old movie. **C**
2. Matt <u>say</u> he memorized the Bible verse. **W**
3. The teacher <u>said</u> the students needed to take their seats. **C**
4. Dan and Chris have <u>seen</u> the Statue of Liberty. **C**
5. Peter <u>see</u> an eye doctor on Wednesday. **W**

Horizons Spelling Grade 3   173

Extended Activities:

1. Ask students to choose two of the spelling words and draw pictures representing those words. Give an opportunity to share their pictures with the class.

2. Have students continue writing sentences for each spelling word in their notebooks.

3. Give students an opportunity to quiz each other on the spelling words and their definitions.

Lesson 109 – Apply Understanding of Words in Writing

Activities:

1. Give the students the page from the *Student Book* for this lesson.

2. Read the directions for the activity on the sheet.

3. As a class, brainstorm activities that students may have done in the past and continue to do or plan to do in the future. Students should keep in mind that they need to draw an accompanying picture.

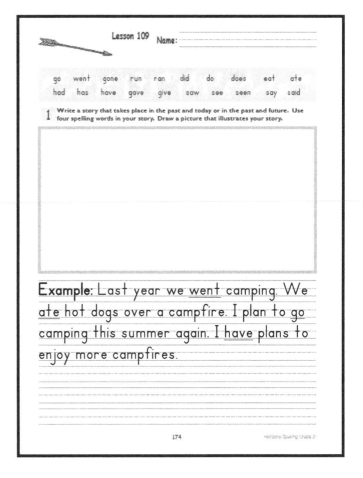

Extended Activities:

1. Share stories.

2. Share pictures.

3. Have the students continue writing sentences for each spelling word in their notebooks.

Lesson 110 – Assess and Evaluate Progress

Activities:

1. Give the students the page from the *Student Book* for this lesson. Tell the students that this is a "Check-up" page to see what they have learned during the week. (Note: Teachers/parents of home schoolers may decide what will be assessed. If a student does exceptionally well on the "What do you know?" pre-assessment, the teacher may choose not to test words already known by the student. Or the teacher may choose to test all words for the week.)

2. Tell students that you will say a word and use it in a sentence. They will listen to the word and the sentence. Then, they will write the word on the line next to the numbers. All challenge words are included in this review.

3. Say the word. Repeat it in the context of a sentence. Repeat the word.

4. The students write the dictated word.

5. The process is repeated until all words have been tested.

6. The teacher may correct in class by writing the words on the board and having the students compare or "self-correct" their work. The teacher may also correct each student's work individually.

7. The teacher then writes any corrections for words misspelled in the space provided.

8. The students study the misspelled words, and practice them on the second side of the Lesson page.

9. Space is provided for retesting, for testing additional sight or "challenge words" added for the week, and for additional practice.

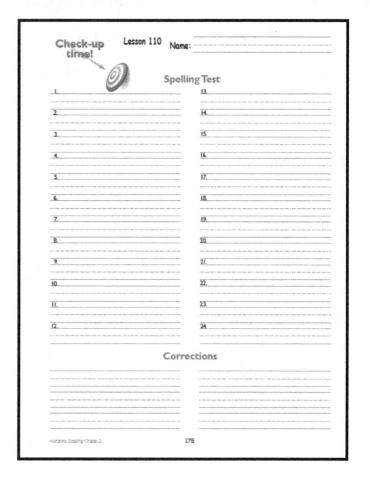

Extended Activity:

Review any words missed. Send words to review home for additional study. Encourage all students in their efforts.

Week 23

Lessons 111-115 — Assess Student's Knowledge

Goal: To review and study prefixes *un*, *re*, *dis* and *pre*.

Review rules:

A prefix is a word part that is added at the beginning of a base word to change the word's meaning or form a new word.

The prefix *un* can mean "not" or "to change something" as in unhappy.

The prefix *re* can mean "back" or "again" as in replay.

The prefix *dis* can mean "away" or "not" as in disorder.

The prefix *pre* can mean "earlier" or "before" as in preview.

What Do You Know?

Give the students the page from the *Student Book* for this lesson. Tell them that this page will be used to see what they currently know about the words for the week. Ask them to listen carefully to each word as you say it, repeat it in a sentence, and say it once again. Follow the procedures for this page as described in the Introduction at the beginning of this *Teacher's Guide*.

Show students how to write their assigned challenge words in the appropriate section at the back of their *Spelling Dictionary*.

Week 23 Worksheet Key

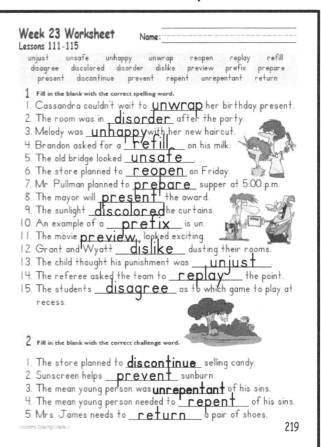

Lesson 111 – Introduce Words

Activities:

1. Give the students the page from the *Student Book* for this lesson.

2. Read to students the directions for the activity sheet.

3. Direct students in completing the challenge word part of the activity sheet.

4. Instruct students to write their assigned challenge words in their *Spelling Dictionaries* in the back section. Words are to be written under the correct letter of the alphabet.

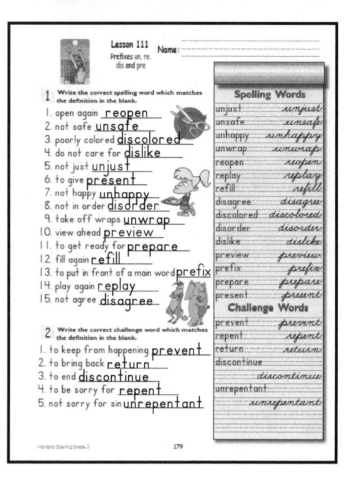

Extended Activities for the Week:

1. Send a list of the week's words home for additional study. You may want to include a letter to the parents urging them to help the students both study and use the words for each week. Emphasize the importance of using spelling words in sentences, in speech, in stories, etc. so that they are given a context and not simply memorized.

2. Challenge students to create lists of additional words with prefixes. They can look for words they encounter in their other subjects or in their free reading.

3. Have students begin the writing of sentences for each spelling word in their notebooks.

4. Assign the reproducible *Week 23 Worksheet* either as homework or as an added classroom activity.

Lesson 112 – Examine and Explore Words

Teaching Tips:

1. Review the prefixes students are working with for the week.

2. Have the class read the list of spelling words together with you.

Activities:

1. Give the students the page from the *Student Book* for this lesson.

2. Review the words in the word box as well as the challenge words.

3. Read the directions with the students. Go over the correct answers as a class.

4. Have students complete the challenge word section of the activity sheet.

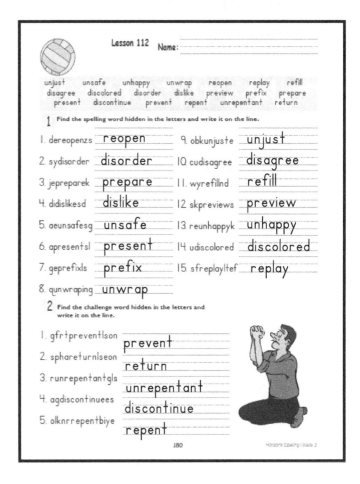

Extended Activities:

1. Ask students if they can think of other words that have prefixes highlighted in the spelling words of the week.

2. Have students continue writing the sentences for each spelling word in their notebooks.

Lesson 113 – Look at Context and Meaning of Words

Teaching Tips:

1. Review words and rules.

2. Give students an opportunity to share any spelling word sentences they have written in their notebooks.

Activities:

1. Give the students the page from the *Student Book* for this lesson.

2. Read the directions on the activity sheet with the students. When they have finished, review the answers as a class.

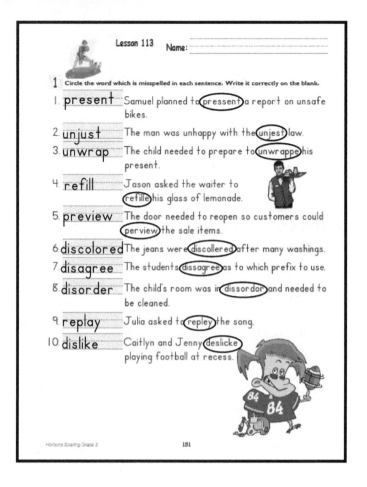

Extended Activities:

1. Write each spelling word forward and backward.

2. Ask students to choose two of the spelling words and draw pictures representing those words. Give an opportunity to share their pictures with the class.

3. Have students continue writing sentences for each spelling word in their notebooks.

4. Give students an opportunity to quiz each other on the spelling words and their definitions.

Lesson 114 – Apply Understanding of Words in Writing

Activities:

1. Give the students the page from the *Student Book* for this lesson.

2. Read the directions for the activity on the sheet.

3. As a class, brainstorm a sentence using a pair of spelling words. This sentence can serve as a model for other sentences.

4. Direct students in writing their sentences.

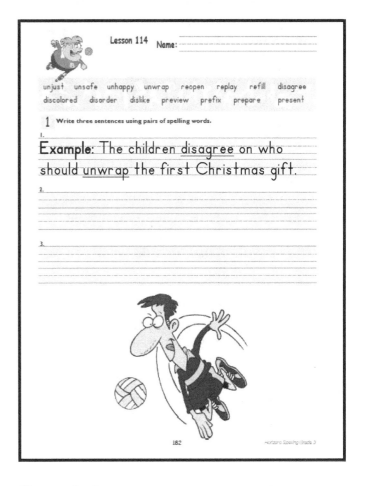

Extended Activities:

1. Have students write their letters in clay or play dough.

2. Share sentences.

3. Have the students continue writing sentences for each spelling word in their notebooks.

Lesson 115 – Assess and Evaluate Progress

Activities:

1. Give the students the page from the *Student Book* for this lesson. Tell the students that this is a "Check-up" page to see what they have learned during the week. (Note: Teachers/parents of home schoolers may decide what will be assessed. If a student does exceptionally well on the "What do you know?" pre-assessment, the teacher may choose not to test words already known by the student. Or the teacher may choose to test all words for the week.)

2. Tell students that you will say a word and use it in a sentence. They will listen to the word and the sentence. Then, they will write the word on the line next to the numbers. All challenge words are included in this review.

3. Say the word. Repeat it in the context of a sentence. Repeat the word.

4. The students write the dictated word.

5. The process is repeated until all words have been tested.

6. The teacher may correct in class by writing the words on the board and having the students compare or "self-correct" their work. The teacher may also correct each student's work individually.

7. The teacher then writes any corrections for words misspelled in the space provided.

8. The students study the misspelled words, and practice them on the second side of the Lesson page.

9. Space is provided for retesting, for testing additional sight or "challenge words" added for the week, and for additional practice.

Lesson 115
Check-up time!

Name: _____

Spelling Test

1. _____   13. _____
2. _____   14. _____
3. _____   15. _____
4. _____   16. _____
5. _____   17. _____
6. _____   18. _____
7. _____   19. _____
8. _____   20. _____
9. _____   21. _____
10. _____   22. _____
11. _____   23. _____
12. _____   24. _____

Corrections

Horizons Spelling Grade 3   183

Extended Activity:

Review any words missed. Send words to review home for additional study. Encourage all students in their efforts.

Week 24 Skill Review

Lessons 116-120 — Once Again for Excellence

Goal: To review words from Lessons 81-115.

Review rules:
Review the rules for Weeks 17-23.

Teacher's Note:

Students will review 28 words each day from the previous seven weeks. All of the words from the previous weeks will be reviewed. None of the challenge words will be reviewed. Students should know that only 28 words will appear on the final test. These words will be taken from Weeks 17-23.

What Do You Remember?

Give the students the page from the *Student Book* for this lesson. Tell them that this page will be used to see what they currently know about the review. Ask them to listen carefully to each word as you say it, repeat it in a sentence, and say it once again. Follow the procedures for this page as described in the Introduction at the beginning of this *Teacher's Guide*. Tell students that the challenge words will not be a part of the review.

Week 24 Worksheet Key

Lesson 116 – Practice Makes Perfect

Activities:

1. Give the students the page from the *Student Book* for this lesson.

2. Read to students the directions for the first activity on the sheet.

3. Direct students in completing the second part of the activity sheet.

Extended Activities for the Week:

1. Send a list of the spelling words from the previous seven weeks home for additional study. Remind parents and students that not all of the spelling words will appear on the final test. You may want to include a letter to the parents urging them to help the students both study and use the words from the previous seven weeks. Emphasize the importance of using spelling words in sentences, in speech, in stories, etc. so that they are given a context and not simply memorized.

2. Assign the reproducible *Week 24 Worksheet* either as homework or as an added classroom activity.

3. Make a chart categorizing the different words students have learned in the pervious seven weeks.

4. You may want to give spot quizzes to check student's spelling of the review words. Emphasize that these are not graded but are being used to help review.

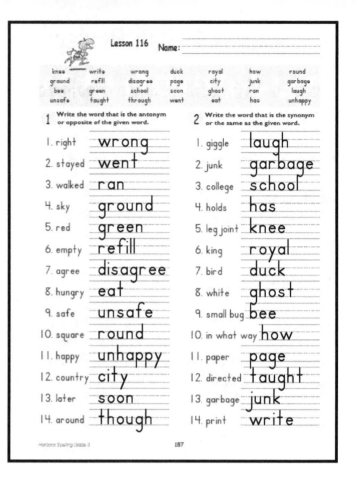

Lesson 117 – Revisit for Success

Activities:

1. Give the students the page from the *Student Book* for this lesson.

2. Review the words in the word box.

3. Read the directions with the students. Once they have completed the activity, go over the answers together.

Extended Activities:

1. Have students take turns quizzing each other on the spelling words in this lesson.

2. Ask students to create a word search using the words in this lesson.

3. You may want to give spot quizzes to check student's spelling of the review words. Emphasize that these are not graded but are being used to help review.

Lesson 118 – Become an Expert

Activities:

1. Give the students the page from the *Student Book* for this lesson.

2. Read the words reviewed in this lesson together as a class.

3. Read the directions for the first section of the activity sheet with the students. When they have finished, review the answers as a class.

4. Have students complete the second half of the activity sheet. Go over those answers as well.

Extended Activities:

1. Have students write the spelling words in this lesson with chalk on a sidewalk. Wash down the sidewalk when you are finished.

2. Ask students to write the words on a piece of paper and outline them in different colors.

3. Challenge students to work individually or with a partner to write a sentence using as many spelling words as they can.

4. You may want to give spot quizzes to check student's spelling of the review words. Emphasize that these are not graded but are being used to help review.

Lesson 119 – Exercise for Mastery

Activities:

1. Give the students the page from the *Student Book* for this lesson.

2. Read the directions for the activity on the sheet.

3. As a class, brainstorm sentences for the first group of words. Students can choose one of these sentences to write on their worksheet.

4. Direct students in writing sentences.

5. Provide time for students to share their sentences.

Extended Activities:

1. Have students write the spelling words for this lesson in shapes such as circles, squares, or ovals.

2. Ask students to write their words adding or subtracting one letter at a time. The words and their parts will form the shape of a pyramid. **Example:**

> w
> wr
> wri
> writ
> write

3. You may want to give spot quizzes to check student's spelling of the review words. Emphasize that these are not graded but are being used to help review.

Lesson 120 – Assess and Evaluate

Activities:

1. Give the students the page from the *Student Book* for this lesson. Tell the students that this is a "Check-up" page to see what they have learned during the week.

2. Tell students that you will say a word and use it in a sentence. They will listen to the word and the sentence. Then, they will write the word on the line next to the numbers.

3. Say the word. Repeat it in the context of a sentence. Repeat the word.

4. The students write the dictated word.

5. The process is repeated until all words have been tested.

6. The teacher may correct in class by writing the words on the board and having the students compare or "self-correct" their work. The teacher may also correct each student's work individually.

7. The teacher then writes any corrections for words misspelled in the space provided.

8. The students study the misspelled words, and practice them on the second side of the Lesson page.

Final Test:

wrap	black	do	squeal
house	found	quick	quiet
oil	discolored	duck	how
circle	press	junk	age
keep	green	bleed	school
ghost	laugh	run	does
prepare	disagree	reopen	eat

Lesson 120
Check-up time!
Name:
Write the words your teacher reads.

1. wrap
2. black
3. do
4. squeal
5. house
6. found
7. quick
8. quiet
9. duck
10. how
11. circle
12. press
13. junk
14. age
15. keep
16. green
17. bleed
18. school
19. ghost
20. laugh
21. run
22. does
23. prepare
24. disagree
25. reopen
26. eat
27. oil
28. discolored

Horizons Spelling Grade 3   191

Extended Activity:

Review any words missed. Send words to review home for additional study. Encourage all students in their efforts.

Week 25

Lessons 121–125 — Assess Student's Knowledge

Goal: To review and study words with the suffixes *ly, ful, ness*.

Review rules:

Most suffixes are added to the end of words and the spelling of the root word does not change.

When a consonant comes before the final *y* of a word, change the *y* to *i* and add the suffix as in *happily*.

When a vowel comes before the final *y*, keep the *y* and add the suffix as in *joyful*.

The suffix *ly* means how often or like as in the words *yearly* or *kindly*.

The suffix *ness* means the state of such as *happiness*.

The suffix *ful* means having or being full or as in *wonderful*.

What Do You Know?

Give the students the page from the *Student Book* for this lesson. Tell them that this page will be used to see what they currently know about the words for the week. Ask them to listen carefully to each word as you say it, repeat it in a sentence, and say it once again. Follow the procedures for this page as described in the Introduction at the beginning of this *Teacher's Guide*.

Show students how to write their assigned challenge words in the appropriate section at the back of their *Spelling Dictionary*.

Week 25 Worksheet Key

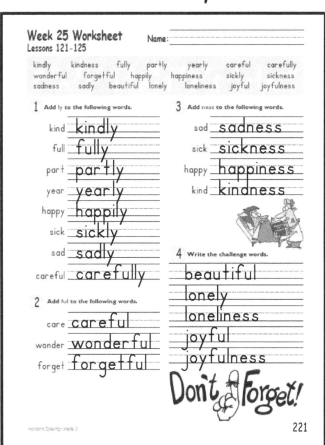

Lesson 121 – Introduce Words

Activities:

1. Give the students the page from the *Student Book* for this lesson.

2. Read to students the directions for the activity on the sheet.

3. Direct students in completing the challenge words section of the activity sheet.

4. Instruct students to write their assigned challenge words in their *Spelling Dictionaries* in the back section. Words are to be written under the correct letter of the alphabet.

Extended Activities for the Week:

1. Send a list of the week's words home for additional study. You may want to include a letter to the parents urging them to help the students both study and use the words for each week. Emphasize the importance of using spelling words in sentences, in speech, in stories, etc. so that they are given a context and not simply memorized.

2. Challenge students to create lists of additional words with *ly*, *ness*, and *ful* suffixes. They can look for words they encounter in their other subjects or in their free reading.

3. Have students begin the writing of sentences for each spelling word in their notebooks.

4. Assign the reproducible *Week 25 Worksheet* either as homework or as an added classroom activity.

Lesson 122 - Examine and Explore Words

Teaching Tips:

1. Review the suffixes students are working with for the week.

2. Have the class read the list of spelling words together with you.

Activities:

1. Give the students the page from the *Student Book* for this lesson.

2. Review the words in the word box as well as the challenge words.

3. Read the directions with the students. Go over any questions students have when they have completed the word search.

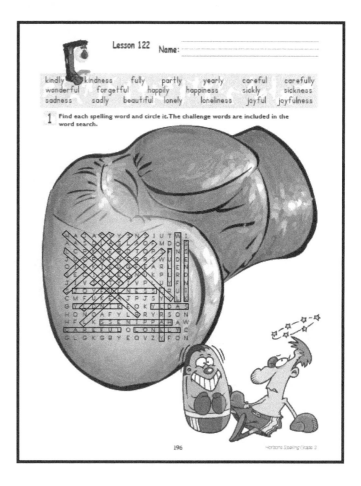

Extended Activities:

1. Ask students to write all of their spelling words in alphabetical order. As an added exercise, have students write their challenge words in reverse alphabetical order.

2. Ask students if they can think of other words that have the prefixes highlighted in the spelling words of the week.

3. Have students continue writing the sentences for each spelling word in their notebooks.

Lesson 123 – Look at Context and Meaning of Words

Teaching Tips:

1. Review words and rules.

2. Give students an opportunity to share any spelling word sentences they have written in their notebooks.

Activities:

1. Give the students the page from the *Student Book* for this lesson.

2. Read the directions on the activity sheet with the students. When they have finished, review the answers as a class.

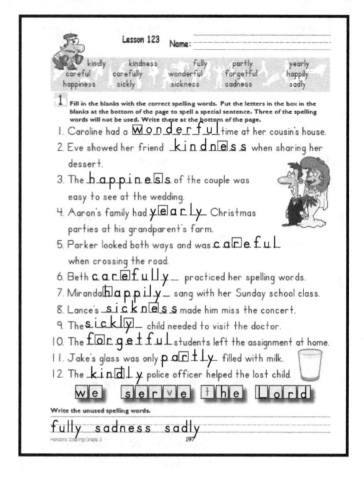

Extended Activities:

1. Ask students to type the spelling words on a computer. Have students use different fonts to make the words look interesting.

2. Ask students to choose two of the spelling words and draw pictures representing those words. Give an opportunity to share their pictures with the class.

3. Have students continue writing sentences for each spelling word in their notebooks.

4. Give students an opportunity to quiz each other on the spelling words and their definitions.

Lesson 124 – Apply Understanding of Words in Writing

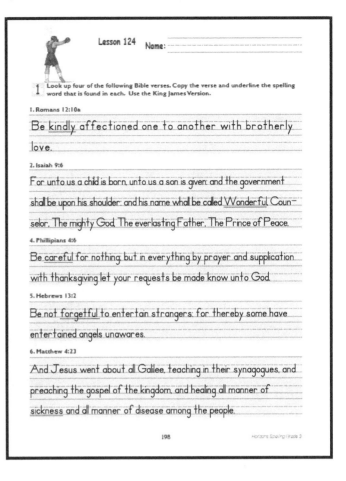

Activities:

1. Give the students the page from the *Student Book* for this lesson. Students should also have their Bibles available. If your students do not have KJV Bibles then prepare and duplicate the needed verses on a handout.

2. Read the directions for the activity on the sheet. You may want to assign students the verses you want them to search. You could also have students work with a partner on the verses.

3. Have students take turns reading the verses and highlighting the spelling words found.

Extended Activities:

1. Ask students to write a letter to a friend or grandparents in which they use four of the spelling words.

2. Have students draw pictures and write their spelling words in the picture.

3. Have the students continue writing sentences for each spelling word in their notebooks.

Lesson 125 – Assess and Evaluate Progress

Activities:

1. Give the students the page from the *Student Book* for this lesson. Tell the students that this is a "Check-up" page to see what they have learned during the week. (Note: Teachers/parents of home schoolers may decide what will be assessed. If a student does exceptionally well on the "What do you know?" pre-assessment, the teacher may choose not to test words already known by the student. Or the teacher may choose to test all words for the week.)

2. Tell students that you will say a word and use it in a sentence. They will listen to the word and the sentence. Then, they will write the word on the line next to the numbers. All challenge words are included in this review.

3. Say the word. Repeat it in the context of a sentence. Repeat the word.

4. The students write the dictated word.

5. The process is repeated until all words have been tested.

6. The teacher may correct in class by writing the words on the board and having the students compare or "self-correct" their work. The teacher may also correct each student's work individually.

7. The teacher then writes any corrections for words misspelled in the space provided.

8. The students study the misspelled words, and practice them on the second side of the Lesson page.

9. Space is provided for retesting, for testing additional sight or "challenge words" added for the week, and for additional practice.

Lesson 125   Name:

Check-up time!

Spelling Test

1.   13.
2.   14.
3.   15.
4.   16.
5.   17.
6.   18.
7.   19.
8.   20.
9.   21.
10.   22.
11.   23.
12.   24.

Corrections

Horizons Spelling Grade 3   199

Extended Activity:

Review any words missed. Send words to review home for additional study. Encourage all students in their efforts.

Week 26

Lessons 126-130 — Assess Student's Knowledge

Goal: To review and study contractions.

Review rules:

Contractions are compound words that have a letter or letters removed as in *cannot* to *can't*.

Contractions use an apostrophe in place of the missing letter or letters as in *it is* to *it's*.

What Do You Know?

Give the students the page from the *Student Book* for this lesson. Tell them that this page will be used to see what they currently know about the words for the week. Ask them to listen carefully to each word as you say it, repeat it in a sentence, and say it once again. Follow the procedures for this page as described in the Introduction at the beginning of this *Teacher's Guide*.

Show students how to write their challenge words in the appropriate section at the back of their *Spelling Dictionary*.

Week 26 Worksheet Key

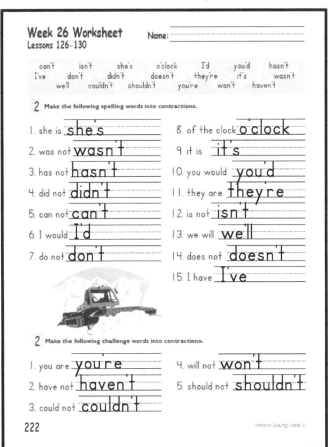

Lesson 126 - Introduce Words

Activities:

1. Give the students the page from the *Student Book* for this lesson.

2. Read to students the directions for the first activity on the sheet.

3. Direct students in completing the second part of the activity sheet.

4. Instruct students to write their assigned challenge words in their *Spelling Dictionaries* in the back section. Words are to be written under the correct letter of the alphabet.

Extended Activities for the Week:

1. Send a list of the week's words home for additional study. You may want to include a letter to the parents urging them to help the students both study and use the words for each week. Emphasize the importance of using spelling words in sentences, in speech, in stories, etc. so that they are given a context and not simply memorized.

2. Challenge students to create lists of additional words with contractions. They can look for words they encounter in their other subjects or in their free reading.

3. Have students begin the writing of sentences for each spelling word in their notebooks.

4. Assign the reproducible *Week 26 Worksheet* either as homework or as an added classroom activity.

Lesson 127 – Examine and Explore Words

Teaching Tips:

1. Review the contractions students are working with for the week.

2. Have the class read the list of spelling words together with you.

Activities:

1. Give the students the page from the *Student Book* for this lesson.

2. Read the directions with the students. Have them choose the contraction spelled correctly in each group.

3. Go over the correct answers when students have completed the activity sheet.

Extended Activities:

1. Ask students if they can think of other words that have contractions highlighted in the spelling words of the week.

2. Have students continue writing the sentences for each spelling word in their notebooks.

Lesson 128 – Look at Context and Meaning of Words

Teaching Tips:

1. Review words and rules.

2. Give students an opportunity to share any spelling word sentences they have written in their notebooks.

Activities:

1. Give the students the page from the *Student Book* for this lesson.

2. Read the directions on the activity sheet with the students. When they have finished, review the answers as a class.

3. Have students complete the challenge word section of the activity sheet. Go over those answers as well.

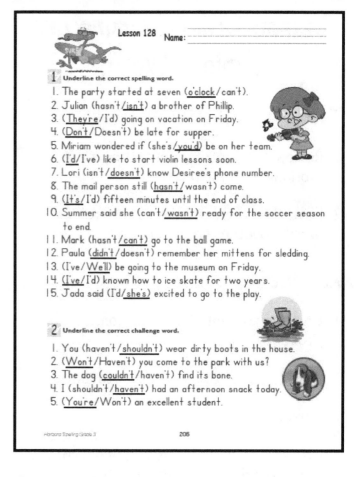

Extended Activities:

1. Ask students to choose two of the spelling words and draw pictures representing those words. Give an opportunity to share their pictures with the class.

2. Have students continue writing sentences for each spelling word in their notebooks.

3. Give students an opportunity to quiz each other on the spelling words and their definitions.

Lesson 129 – Apply Understanding of Words in Writing

Activities:

1. Give the students the page from the *Student Book* for this lesson.

2. Read the directions for the activity sheet.

3. As a class, discuss the picture on the page. Talk about how the spelling words might be used to describe the picture.

4. Direct students in completing the activity sheet.

Extended Activities:

1. Share stories.

2. Share pictures.

3. Have the students continue writing sentences for each spelling word in their notebooks.

Lesson 130 – Assess and Evaluate Progress

Activities:

1. Give the students the page from the *Student Book* for this lesson. Tell the students that this is a "Check-up" page to see what they have learned during the week. (Note: Teachers/parents of home schoolers may decide what will be assessed. If a student does exceptionally well on the "What do you know?" pre-assessment, the teacher may choose not to test words already known by the student. Or the teacher may choose to test all words for the week.)

2. Tell students that you will say a word and use it in a sentence. They will listen to the word and the sentence. Then, they will write the word on the line next to the numbers. All challenge words are included in this review.

3. Say the word. Repeat it in the context of a sentence. Repeat the word.

4. The students write the dictated word.

5. The process is repeated until all words have been tested.

6. The teacher may correct in class by writing the words on the board and having the students compare or "self-correct" their work. The teacher may also correct each student's work individually.

7. The teacher then writes any corrections for words misspelled in the space provided.

8. The students study the misspelled words, and practice them on the second side of the Lesson page.

9. Space is provided for retesting, for testing additional sight or "challenge words" added for the week, and for additional practice.

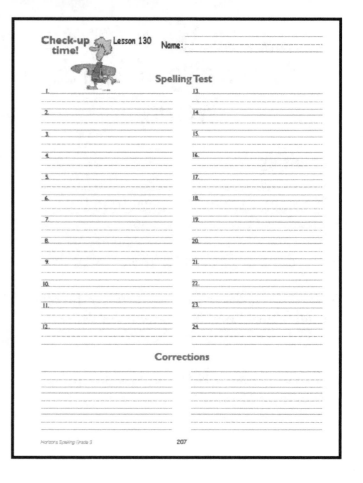

Extended Activity:

Review any words missed. Send words to review home for additional study. Encourage all students in their efforts.

Week 27

Lessons 131-135 — Assess Student's Knowledge

Goal: To review and study words with more than one syllable.

Review rules:

In words where there is a vowel followed by two consonants and then another vowel, the word is divided between the two consonants. **Examples** include the words *sister* and *monkey*: *sis/ter; mon/key*.

In words where there are double consonants, the syllables are divided between the two consonants. **Examples** include *letter* and *yellow*: *let/ter; yel/low*.

What Do You Know?

Give the students the page from the *Student Book* for this lesson. Tell them that this page will be used to see what they currently know about the words for the week. Ask them to listen carefully to each word as you say it, repeat it in a sentence, and say it once again. Follow the procedures for this page as described in the Introduction at the beginning of this *Teacher's Guide*.

Show students how to write their assigned challenge words in the appropriate section at the back of their *Spelling Dictionary*.

Week 27 Worksheet Key

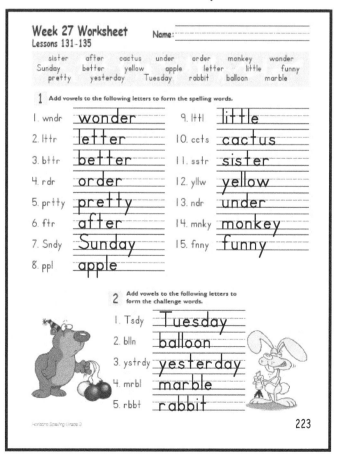

Lesson 131 – Introduce Words

Activities:

1. Give the students the page from the *Student Book* for this lesson.

2. Read to students the directions for the activity on the sheet.

3. Direct students in completing each matching section of the activity.

4. Instruct students to write their assigned challenge words in their *Spelling Dictionaries* in the back section. Words are to be written under the correct letter of the alphabet.

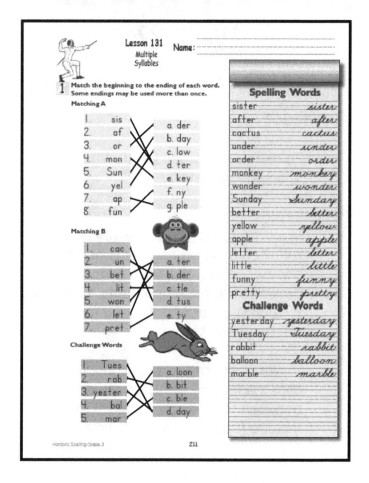

Extended Activities for the Week:

1. Send a list of the week's words home for additional study. You may want to include a letter to the parents urging them to help the students both study and use the words for each week. Emphasize the importance of using spelling words in sentences, in speech, in stories, etc. so that they are given a context and not simply memorized.

2. Challenge students to create lists of additional words with more than one syllable that follow the rules in this lesson. They can look for words they encounter in their other subjects or in their free reading. Maybe some of the students' names follow these rules.

3. Have students begin the writing of sentences for each spelling word in their notebooks.

4. Assign the reproducible *Week 27 Worksheet* either as homework or as an added classroom activity.

Lesson 132 – Examine and Explore Words

Teaching Tips:

1. Review the words students are working with for the week.

2. Have the class read the list of spelling words together with you.

Activities:

1. Give the students the page from the *Student Book* for this lesson.

2. Read the directions with the students. Direct them in dividing the words into two syllables. You may want to do the first one as an example.

3. After students have completed the exercise, go over the answers together as a class.

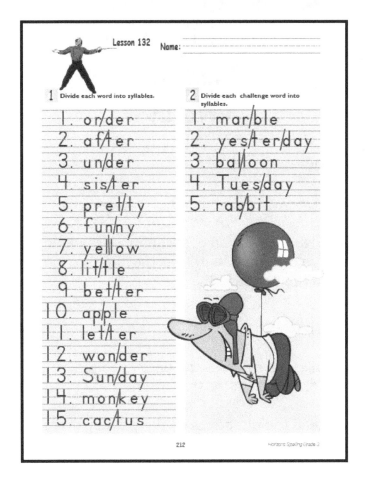

Extended Activities:

1. Have students work together to see how many of the words they can find in a newspaper page.

2. Have students continue writing the sentences for each spelling word in their notebooks.

Lesson 133 – Look at Context and Meaning of Words

Teaching Tips:

1. Review words and rules.

2. Give students an opportunity to share any spelling word sentences they have written in their notebooks.

Activities:

1. Give the students the page from the *Student Book* for this lesson.

2. Read the directions on the activity sheet with the students. When they have finished, review the answers as a class.

3. Have students complete the challenge word section of the activity sheet. Go over those answers as well.

Lesson 133   Name:

sister	after	cactus	under	order	monkey	wonder
Sunday	better	yellow	apple	letter	little	funny
pretty	yesterday	Tuesday	rabbit	balloon	marble

1 Fill in the blank with the with the best spelling word.
1. Grace hurt her finger when touching a **cactus**.
2. The soccer team had a **better** record than last year.
3. Mr. Perry planned to **order** a pizza.
4. Charlie went to church on **Sunday**.
5. Scarlett picked an **apple** from the tree.
6. Olivia has a **sister** named Jessica.
7. Lucas has a **little** brother.
8. Georgia received a **pretty** dress for her birthday.
9. Thomas found the frisbee **under** the bush.
10. Isabel's room was painted **yellow**.
11. Jack chased **after** the soccer ball.
12. Sophia told a **funny** story.
13. Kyle wrote a **letter** to his grandpa.
14. Ruby and Emily **wonder** when lunch will be served.
15. Oliver saw a **monkey** at the zoo.

2 Fill in the blank with the best challenge word.
1. Jake had a piano lesson **yesterday**.
2. The red **balloon** floated to the ceiling.
3. Lucy planned to play at Lily's house on **Tuesday**.
4. The **rabbit** hopped across the yard.
5. The **marble** rolled underneath the couch.

Horizons Spelling Grade 3   213

Extended Activities:

1. Ask students to choose two of the spelling words and draw pictures representing those words. Give an opportunity to share their pictures with the class.

2. Have students continue writing sentences for each spelling word in their notebooks.

3. Give students an opportunity to quiz each other on the spelling words and their definitions.

Lesson 134 – Apply Understanding of Words in Writing

Activities:

1. Give the students the page from the *Student Book* for this lesson.

2. Read the directions for the activity on the sheet.

3. As a class, brainstorm ways in which you might use the spelling words to describe the zoo scene.

4. Direct students in completing the activity sheet.

Extended Activities:

1. Share stories.

2. Ask students to draw their own zoo scenes.

3. Have the students continue writing sentences for each spelling word in their notebooks.

Lesson 135 - Assess and Evaluate Progress

Activities:

1. Give the students the page from the *Student Book* for this lesson. Tell the students that this is a "Check-up" page to see what they have learned during the week. (Note: Teachers/parents of home schoolers may decide what will be assessed. If a student does exceptionally well on the "What do you know?" pre-assessment, the teacher may choose not to test words already known by the student. Or the teacher may choose to test all words for the week.)

2. Tell students that you will say a word and use it in a sentence. They will listen to the word and the sentence. Then, they will write the word on the line next to the numbers. All challenge words are included in this review.

3. Say the word. Repeat it in the context of a sentence. Repeat the word.

4. The students write the dictated word.

5. The process is repeated until all words have been tested.

6. The teacher may correct in class by writing the words on the board and having the students compare or "self-correct" their work. The teacher may also correct each student's work individually.

7. The teacher then writes any corrections for words misspelled in the space provided.

8. The students study the misspelled words, and practice them on the second side of the Lesson page.

9. Space is provided for retesting, for testing additional sight or "challenge words" added for the week, and for additional practice.

Extended Activity:

Review any words missed. Send words to review home for additional study. Encourage all students in their efforts.

Lesson 135   Name:

Check-up time!

Spelling Test

1. _____ 13. _____
2. _____ 14. _____
3. _____ 15. _____
4. _____ 16. _____
5. _____ 17. _____
6. _____ 18. _____
7. _____ 19. _____
8. _____ 20. _____
9. _____ 21. _____
10. _____ 22. _____
11. _____ 23. _____
12. _____ 24. _____

Corrections

Horizons Spelling Grade 3   215

164   *Horizons Spelling Grade 3*

Week 28

Lessons 136-140 — Assess Student's Knowledge

Goal: To review and study words ending in *ing* and *ed*.

Review rule:

A word ending in a vowel plus a consonant doubles the final consonant before adding *ing* and *ed*. **Examples** include the words *stopped* and *swimming*.

What Do You Know?

Give the students the page from the *Student Book* for this lesson. Tell them that this page will be used to see what they currently know about the words for the week. Ask them to listen carefully to each word as you say it, repeat it in a sentence, and say it once again. Follow the procedures for this page as described in the Introduction at the beginning of this *Teacher's Guide*.

Show students how to write their assigned challenge words in the appropriate section at the back of their *Spelling Dictionary*.

Week 28 Worksheet Key

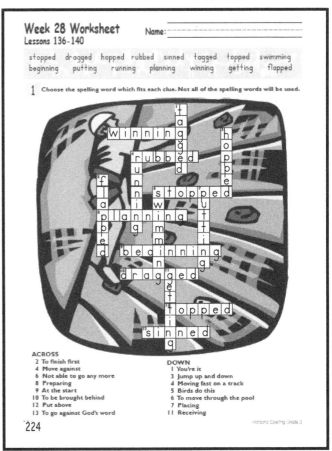

Lesson 136 – Introduce Words

Activities:

1. Give the students the page from the *Student Book* for this lesson.

2. Read to students the directions for the first activity on the sheet.

3. Direct students in completing the other parts of the activity sheet.

4. Instruct students to write their assigned Challenge Words in their *Spelling Dictionaries* in the back section. Words are to be written under the correct letter of the alphabet.

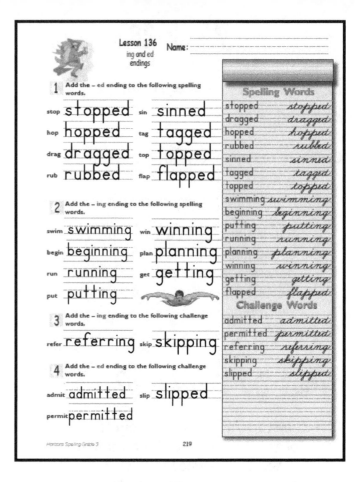

Extended Activities for the Week:

1. Send a list of the week's words home for additional study. You may want to include a letter to the parents urging them to help the students both study and use the words for each week. Emphasize the importance of using spelling words in sentences, in speech, in stories, etc. so that they are given a context and not simply memorized.

2. Challenge students to create lists of additional words that end in a vowel and consonant and add *ing* or *ed*. They can look for words they encounter in their other subjects or in their free reading.

3. Have students begin the writing of sentences for each spelling word in their notebooks.

4. Assign the reproducible *Week 28 Worksheet* either as homework or as an added classroom activity.

Lesson 137 – Examine and Explore Words

Teaching Tips:

1. Review the spelling words students are working with for the week.

2. Have the class read the list of spelling words together with you.

Activities:

1. Give the students the page from the *Student Book* for this lesson.

2. Review the words in the word box as well as the challenge words.

3. Read the directions with the students. Have them complete the top portion of the activity sheet. Go over the correct answers as a class.

4. Have students complete the challenge word section of the sheet. Go over these answers as well.

Extended Activities:

1. Ask students if they can think of other words that have *ing* and *ed* endings that follow the rule for doubling the final consonant.

2. Have students continue writing the sentences for each spelling word in their notebooks.

Lesson 138 - Look at Context and Meaning of Words

Teaching Tips:

1. Review words and rules.

2. Give students an opportunity to share any spelling word sentences they have written in their notebooks.

Activities:

1. Give the students the page from the *Student Book* for this lesson.

2. Read the directions on the activity sheet with the students. When they have finished, review the answers as a class.

3. Have students complete the bottom half of the activity sheet. Go over those answers as well.

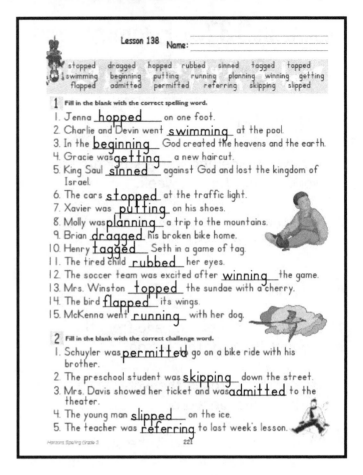

Extended Activities:

1. Ask students to choose two of the spelling words and draw pictures representing those words. Give an opportunity to share their pictures with the class.

2. Have students continue writing sentences for each spelling word in their notebooks.

3. Give students an opportunity to quiz each other on the spelling words and their definitions.

Lesson 139 – Apply Understanding of Words in Writing

Activities:

1. Give the students the page from the *Student Book* for this lesson.

2. Read the directions for the first activity on the sheet.

3. As a class, brainstorm a sentence students could write using two of the spelling words. Discuss as well what kind of picture could accompany the sentence.

4. Direct students in completing the activity.

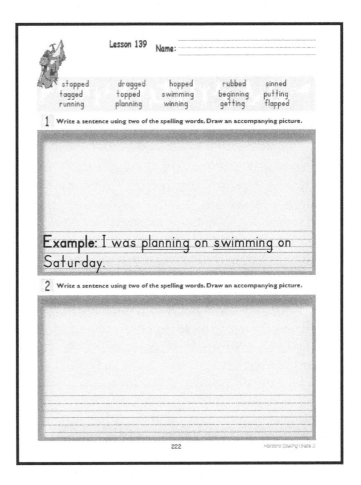

Extended Activities:

1. Share stories.

2. Share pictures.

3. Have the students continue writing sentences for each spelling word in their notebooks.

Lesson 140 – Assess and Evaluate Progress

Activities:

1. Give the students the page from the *Student Book* for this lesson. Tell the students that this is a "Check-up" page to see what they have learned during the week. (Note: Teachers/parents of home schoolers may decide what will be assessed. If a student does exceptionally well on the "What do you know?" pre-assessment, the teacher may choose not to test words already known by the student. Or the teacher may choose to test all words for the week.)

2. Tell students that you will say a word and use it in a sentence. They will listen to the word and the sentence. Then, they will write the word on the line next to the numbers. All challenge words are included in this review.

3. Say the word. Repeat it in the context of a sentence. Repeat the word.

4. The students write the dictated word.

5. The process is repeated until all words have been tested.

6. The teacher may correct in class by writing the words on the board and having the students compare or "self-correct" their work. The teacher may also correct each student's work individually.

7. The teacher then writes any corrections for words misspelled in the space provided.

8. The students study the misspelled words, and practice them on the second side of the Lesson page.

9. Space is provided for retesting, for testing additional sight or "challenge words" added for the week, and for additional practice.

Lesson 140   Name:

Check-up time!

Spelling Test

1.   13.
2.   14.
3.   15.
4.   16.
5.   17.
6.   18.
7.   19.
8.   20.
9.   21.
10.   22.
11.   23.
12.   24.

Corrections

Horizons Spelling Grade 3   223

Extended Activity:

Review any words missed. Send words to review home for additional study. Encourage all students in their efforts.

Week 29

Lessons 141-145 — Assess Student's Knowledge

Goal: To review and study compound words.

Review rules:

There are three types of compound words:

A hyphenated compound word is two words joined by a hyphen.

An open compound word is two closely associated words with no adjoining punctuation.

A closed compound is two or more words joined as one solid word.

What Do You Know?

Give the students the page from the *Student Book* for this lesson. Tell them that this page will be used to see what they currently know about the words for the week. Ask them to listen carefully to each word as you say it, repeat it in a sentence, and say it once again. Follow the procedures for this page as described in the Introduction at the beginning of this *Teacher's Guide*.

Show students how to write their assigned Challenge Words in the appropriate section at the back of their *Spelling Dictionary*.

What do you know? Lessons 141-145   Name: _____

Words for the Week

1. myself
2. anything
3. crossword
4. bedroom
5. butterfly
6. homework
7. wallpaper
8. grandparents
9. sister-in-law
10. good-bye
11. nine-year-old
12. post office
13. good-looking
14. family-tree
15. police officer
16. childlike
17. washing machine
18. handkerchief
19. stagecoach
20. best-selling

Practice

Horizons Spelling Grade 3   225

Week 29 Worksheet Key

Week 29 Worksheet   Name: _____
Lessons 141-145

myself anything crossword bedroom butterfly homework wallpaper grandparents sister-in-law good-bye nine-year-old post office good-looking family-tree police officer **challenge words** childlike washing machine handkerchief stagecoach best-selling

1 List the spelling words which are hyphenated compounds.

sister-in-law   good-bye   nine-year-old   good-looking   family-tree

2 List the spelling words which are open compounds.

post office   police officer

3 List the spelling words which are closed compounds.

myself   anything   crossword   bedroom   homework   grandparents   wallpaper   butterfly

4 List the challenge words which are hyphenated compounds.

best-selling

5 List the challenge words which are open compounds.

washing machine

6 List the challenge words which are closed compounds.

childlike   handkerchief   stagecoach

Horizons Spelling Grade 3   225

Lesson 141 – Introduce Words

Activities:

1. Give the students the page from the *Student Book* for this lesson.

2. Read to students the directions for the activity on the sheet.

3. Direct students in completing the other parts of the activity sheet.

4. Instruct students to write their assigned Challenge Words in their *Spelling Dictionaries* in the back section. Words are to be written under the correct letter of the alphabet.

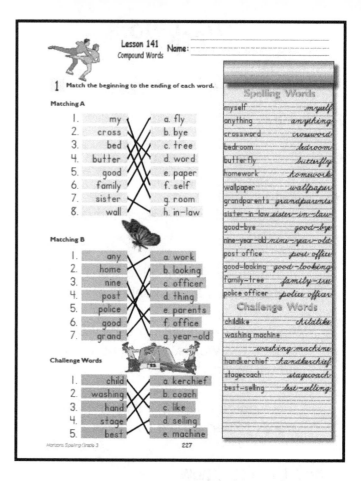

Extended Activities for the Week:

1. Send a list of the week's words home for additional study. You may want to include a letter to the parents urging them to help the students both study and use the words for each week. Emphasize the importance of using spelling words in sentences, in speech, in stories, etc. so that they are given a context and not simply memorized.

2. Challenge students to create lists of additional compound words. They can look for words they encounter in their other subjects or in their free reading.

3. Have students begin the writing of sentences for each spelling word in their notebooks.

4. Assign the reproducible *Week 29 Worksheet* either as homework or as an added classroom activity.

Lesson 142 – Examine and Explore Words

Teaching Tips:

1. Review the compound words students are working with for the week.

2. Have the class read the list of spelling words together with you.

Activities:

1. Give the students the page from the *Student Book* for this lesson.

2. Read the directions with the students. Go over the answers as a class.

Extended Activities:

1. Ask students if they can think of other words that have compounds highlighted in the spelling words of the week.

2. Have students continue writing the sentences for each spelling word in their notebooks.

Lesson 143 - Look at Context and Meaning of Words

Teaching Tips:

1. Review words and rules.

2. Give students an opportunity to share any spelling word sentences they have written in their notebooks.

Activities:

1. Give the students the page from the *Student Book* for this lesson.

2. Read the directions on the activity sheet with the students. When they have finished, review the answers as a class.

Lesson 143   Name: _____

myself	anything	crossword	butterfly	bedroom
homework	wallpaper	grandparents	sister-in-law	good-bye
nine-year-old	post office	good-looking	family-tree	police officer
childlike	washing machine	handkerchief	stagecoach	best-selling

1 Fill in the blank with the correct spelling word.

1. Mason completed the **crossword** puzzle.
2. Maya helped her mom **wallpaper** the room.
3. The teacher said **good-bye** to her students at the end of the day.
4. Owen slept in a blue **bedroom**.
5. Brendan thought the beagle was **good-looking**.
6. Austin was excited to see his **grandparents**.
7. Morgan's father is a **police officer**.
8. I made the bed **myself**.
9. Zoe said she didn't have any **homework**.
10. Arianna brought a letter to the **post office**.
11. My mom's brother and **sister-in-law** are coming to visit.
12. Elliot needed to ask his great-grandmother questions about her relatives for the **family-tree** project.
13. MacKenzie said she didn't have **anything** to do.
14. Hunter would be a **nine-year-old** on his next birthday.
15. The **butterfly** landed on the flower.

2 Fill in the blank with the correct challenge word.

1. Mrs. Tyson put the dirty clothes in the **washing machine**.
2. Because he had a cold, Mr. Eliot put a **handkerchief** in his pocket.
3. Grandpa Smith had a **childlike** excitement for amusement parks.
4. In the old west, people traveled by **stagecoach**.
5. The store sold the **best-selling** book.

Horizons Spelling Grade 3   229

Extended Activities:

1. Ask students to choose two of the spelling words and draw pictures representing those words. Give an opportunity to share their pictures with the class.

2. Have students continue writing sentences for each spelling word in their notebooks.

3. Give students an opportunity to quiz each other on the spelling words and their definitions.

Lesson 144 – Apply Understanding of Words in Writing

Activities:

1. Give the students the page from the *Student Book* for this lesson.

2. Read the directions for the activity on the sheet.

3. As a class, brainstorm sentences for the first group of spelling words.

4. Direct students in completing the activity sheet and drawing pictures.

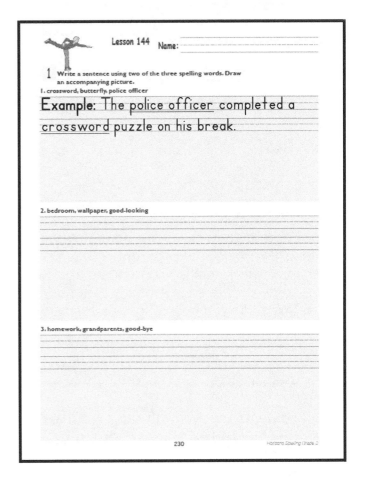

Extended Activities:

1. Share sentences.

2. Share pictures.

3. Have the students continue writing sentences for each spelling word in their notebooks.

Lesson 145 – Assess and Evaluate Progress

Activities:

1. Give the students the page from the *Student Book* for this lesson. Tell the students that this is a "Check-up" page to see what they have learned during the week. (Note: Teachers/parents of home schoolers may decide what will be assessed. If a student does exceptionally well on the "What do you know?" pre-assessment, the teacher may choose not to test words already known by the student. Or the teacher may choose to test all words for the week.)

2. Tell students that you will say a word and use it in a sentence. They will listen to the word and the sentence. Then, they will write the word on the line next to the numbers. All challenge words are included in this review.

3. Say the word. Repeat it in the context of a sentence. Repeat the word.

4. The students write the dictated word.

5. The process is repeated until all words have been tested.

6. The teacher may correct in class by writing the words on the board and having the students compare or "self-correct" their work. The teacher may also correct each student's work individually.

7. The teacher then writes any corrections for words misspelled in the space provided.

8. The students study the misspelled words, and practice them on the second side of the Lesson page.

9. Space is provided for retesting, for testing additional sight or "challenge words" added for the week, and for additional practice.

Check-up time!

Lesson 145   Name:

Spelling Test

1.   13.
2.   14.
3.   15.
4.   16.
5.   17.
6.   18.
7.   19.
8.   20.
9.   21.
10.   22.
11.   23.
12.   24.

Corrections

Horizons Spelling Grade 3   231

Extended Activity:

Review any words missed. Send words to review home for additional study. Encourage all students in their efforts.

Week 30

Lessons 146-150 — Assess Student's Knowledge

Goal: To review and study words with the *ea* vowel combinations.

Review rules:

The *ea* vowel combination can be sounded $\bar{e}$ as in *mean*, $\breve{e}$ as in *deaf*, $\bar{a}$ as in *great*, $\hat{a}$ as in *wear*, and $\hat{u}$ as in *learn*.

What Do You Know?

Give the students the page from the *Student Book* for this lesson. Tell them that this page will be used to see what they currently know about the words for the week. Ask them to listen carefully to each word as you say it, repeat it in a sentence, and say it once again. Follow the procedures for this page as described in the Introduction at the beginning of this *Teacher's Guide*.

Show students how to write their assigned Challenge Words in the appropriate section at the back of their *Spelling Dictionary*.

Week 30 Worksheet Key

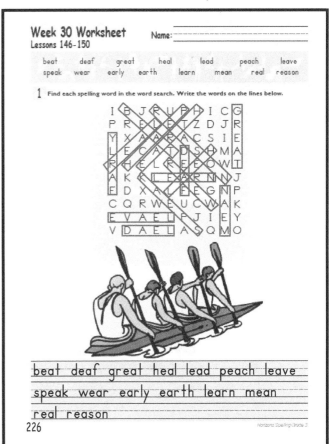

Lesson 146 – Introduce Words

Activities:

1. Give the students the page from the *Student Book* for this lesson.

2. Read to students the directions for the activity on the sheet.

3. Instruct students to write their assigned Challenge Words in their *Spelling Dictionaries* in the back section. Words are to be written under the correct letter of the alphabet.

Extended Activities for the Week:

1. Send a list of the week's words home for additional study. You may want to include a letter to the parents urging them to help the students both study and use the words for each week. Emphasize the importance of using spelling words in sentences, in speech, in stories, etc. so that they are given a context and not simply memorized.

2. Challenge students to create lists of additional words with *ea* vowel combinations. They can look for words they encounter in their other subjects or in their free reading.

3. Have students begin the writing of sentences for each spelling word in their notebooks.

4. Assign the reproducible *Week 30 Worksheet* either as homework or as an added classroom activity.

Lesson 147 – Examine and Explore Words

Teaching Tips:

1. Review the *ea* vowel combinations students are working with for the week.

2. Have the class read the list of spelling words together with you.

Activities:

1. Give the students the page from the *Student Book* for this lesson.

2. Read the directions with the students. Instruct the students to read each row of words and to circle the word that is spelled incorrectly.

3. You can extend the activity by having students write the misspelled words correctly on a sheet of paper.

4. Go over the correct responses after students have completed the activity.

Extended Activities:

1. Have students write each of their spelling words three times using three different color crayons.

2. Ask students if they can think of other words that have *ea* highlighted in the spelling words of the week.

3. Have students continue writing the sentences for each spelling word in their notebooks.

Lesson 148 – Look at Context and Meaning of Words

Teaching Tips:

1. Review words and rules.

2. Give students an opportunity to share any spelling word sentences they have written in their notebooks.

Activities:

1. Give the students the page from the *Student Book* for this lesson.

2. Read the directions on the activity sheet with the students. When they have finished, review the answers as a class.

3. Have students complete the challenge word portion of the activity sheet. Go over those answers as well.

Lesson 148   Name: _____

beat   deaf   great   heal   lead   peach
leave   speak   wear   early   earth   learn   mean
real   reason   creation   heaven   measure   season   weapon

1 Fill in the blank with the correct spelling word.
1. The doctor said the child's broken bone would take a long time to **heal**.
2. Carrie ate a fresh **peach**.
3. Eli helped his dad plant bean seeds in the **earth**.
4. The musician **beat** the drum.
5. The congregation was asked to **leave** through the center aisle.
6. Julia wanted a **real** dog and not a toy one.
7. The child was so surprised by his birthday party he couldn't **speak**.
8. The runner took the **lead** at the end of the race.
9. The **deaf** student signed for the church service.
10. The **reason** we celebrate Christmas is because of Jesus' birth.
11. The teen was eager to **learn** to drive.
12. George Washington was a **great** general.
13. Jenna left **early** for school.
14. The **mean** dog growled at the visitor.
15. Jonas wanted to **wear** his new shoes.

2 Fill in the blank with the correct challenge word.
1. The knight used a sword as a **weapon**.
2. Patrick enjoyed spending time in God's **creation**.
3. The carpenter needed to **measure** the door.
4. Mara's favorite **season** is fall.
5. In the beginning God created **heaven** and earth.

Horizons Spelling Grade 3   237

Extended Activities:

1. Ask students to choose two of the spelling words and draw pictures representing those words. Give an opportunity to share their pictures with the class.

2. Have students continue writing sentences for each spelling word in their notebooks.

3. Give students an opportunity to quiz each other on the spelling words and their definitions.

Lesson 149 – Apply Understanding of Words in Writing

Activities:

1. Give the students the page from the *Student Book* for this lesson.

2. Read the directions for the activity on the sheet.

3. As a class, review some of the miracles Jesus' performed

4. Direct students in completing the activity sheet.

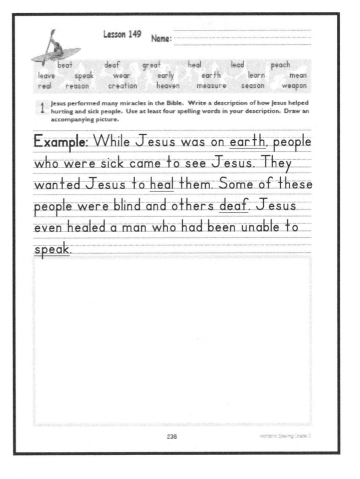

Extended Activities:

1. Share sentences.

2. Share pictures.

3. Have the students continue writing sentences for each spelling word in their notebooks.

Lesson 150 – Assess and Evaluate Progress

Activities:

1. Give the students the page from the *Student Book* for this lesson. Tell the students that this is a "Check-up" page to see what they have learned during the week. (Note: Teachers/parents of home schoolers may decide what will be assessed. If a student does exceptionally well on the "What do you know?" pre-assessment, the teacher may choose not to test words already known by the student. Or the teacher may choose to test all words for the week.)

2. Tell students that you will say a word and use it in a sentence. They will listen to the word and the sentence. Then, they will write the word on the line next to the numbers. All challenge words are included in this review.

3. Say the word. Repeat it in the context of a sentence. Repeat the word.

4. The students write the dictated word.

5. The process is repeated until all words have been tested.

6. The teacher may correct in class by writing the words on the board and having the students compare or "self-correct" their work. The teacher may also correct each student's work individually.

7. The teacher then writes any corrections for words misspelled in the space provided.

8. The students study the misspelled words, and practice them on the second side of the Lesson page.

9. Space is provided for retesting, for testing additional sight or "challenge words" added for the week, and for additional practice.

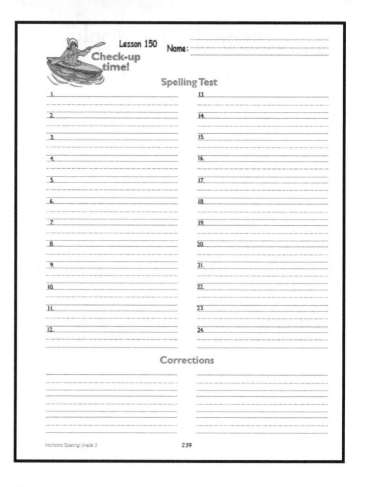

Extended Activity:

Review any words missed. Send words to review home for additional study. Encourage all students in their efforts.

Horizons Spelling Grade 3

Week 31

Lessons 151-155 — Assess Student's Knowledge

Goal: To review and study words ending in a silent *e*

Review rules:

A vowel is generally long if it is followed by a consonant and silent *e* as in *dime*.

A vowel is generally short if it is followed by the consonant *r* and a silent *e* as in *stare*.

What Do You Know?

Give the students the page from the *Student Book* for this lesson. Tell them that this page will be used to see what they currently know about the words for the week. Ask them to listen carefully to each word as you say it, repeat it in a sentence, and say it once again. Follow the procedures for this page as described in the Introduction at the beginning of this *Teacher's Guide*.

Show students how to write their assigned Challenge Words in the appropriate section at the back of their *Spelling Dictionary*.

What do you know? Lessons 151-155 Name: _____

Words for the Week

1. done	11. pane
2. come	12. pride
3. some	13. rinse
4. bite	14. serve
5. care	15. bike
6. dime	16. whistle
7. mice	17. uncle
8. mine	18. feline
9. state	19. gasoline
10. stare	20. divide

Practice

Week 31 Worksheet Key

Week 31 Worksheet Lessons 151-155   Name: _____

done come some bite care dime mice mine state stare pane
pride rinse serve bike whistle uncle feline gasoline divide

1 Underline the misspelled word in each sentence. Write the word correctly
1. Victoria rode her bike with <u>peride</u>. **pride**

2. Mrs. Hunter washed and rinsed the <u>pain</u> of glass. **pane**

3. Mr. Walker said he was <u>doun</u> with supper and couldn't eat one more bite. **done**

4. Mrs. Penn was not happy to find some <u>meece</u> in her home. **mice**

5. Ryan said, "That dime is <u>minne</u>. **mine**

6. Logan planned to <u>seurve</u> his family their meal. **serve**

7. Ella planned to <u>cume</u> to Hannah's birthday party. **come**

8. Noah planned to take good <u>caere</u> of his new bike. **care**

9. Elijah stared at the <u>staet</u> map. **state**

2 Underline the misspelled challenge word in each sentence. Write the word correctly.
1. Tony's uncle taught him to <u>wistle</u> **whistle**

2. Mrs. Marshall planned to <u>devide</u> the last piece of pizza in half. **divide**

3. The <u>felline</u> did not like the smell of gasoline. **feline**

Lesson 151 – Introduce Words

Activities:

1. Give the students the page from the *Student Book* for this lesson.

2. Read to students the directions for the first activity on the sheet.

3. Direct students in completing the challenge word section of the activity sheet.

4. Instruct students to write their assigned Challenge Words in their *Spelling Dictionaries* in the back section. Words are to be written under the correct letter of the alphabet.

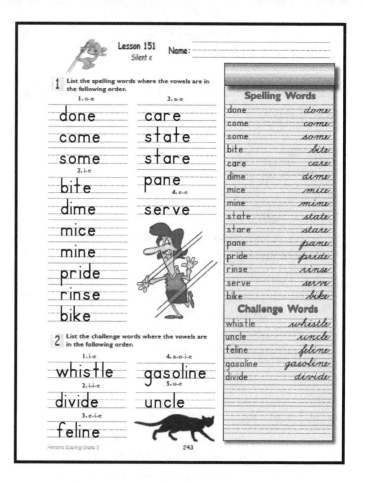

Extended Activities for the Week:

1. Send a list of the week's words home for additional study. You may want to include a letter to the parents urging them to help the students both study and use the words for each week. Emphasize the importance of using spelling words in sentences, in speech, in stories, etc. so that they are given a context and not simply memorized.

2. Challenge students to create lists of additional words ending with silent e's. They can look for words they encounter in their other subjects or in their free reading.

3. Have students begin the writing of sentences for each spelling word in their notebooks.

4. Assign the reproducible *Week 31 Worksheet* either as homework or as an added classroom activity.

Lesson 152 – Examine and Explore Words

Teaching Tips:

1. Review the silent *e* words students are working with for the week.

2. Have the class read the list of spelling words together with you.

Activities:

1. Give the students the page from the *Student Book* for this lesson.

2. Review the words in the word box as well as the challenge words.

3. Read the directions with the students. When they have completed the crossword, go over the answers together as a class.

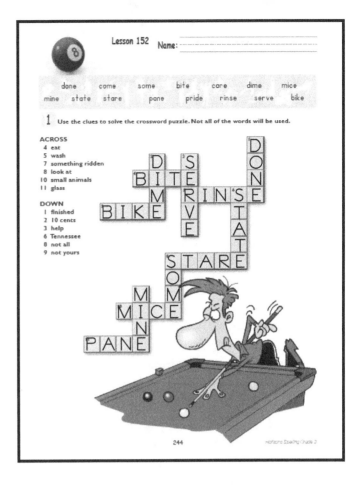

Extended Activities:

1. Ask students if they can think of other words that have a silent *e* at the end.

2. Have students continue writing the sentences for each spelling word in their notebooks.

Lesson 153 – Look at Context and Meaning of Words

Teaching Tips:

1. Review words and rules.

2. Give students an opportunity to share any spelling word sentences they have written in their notebooks.

Activities:

1. Give the students the page from the *Student Book* for this lesson.

2. Read the directions on the activity sheet with the students. When they have finished, review the answers as a class.

3. Have students complete the challenge word section of the activity sheet. Go over those answers as well.

Lesson 153   Name:

done come some bite care dime mice mine state store pane
pride rinse serve bike whistle uncle feline gasoline divide

1 Choose the spelling word that best completes each sentence.
1. The church planned projects to **serve** others.
2. Sydney took a **bite** from her sandwich.
3. Alexa's dog will **come** when called.
4. Mrs. Nader needed to **rinse** the baby's bottle.
5. The **mice** chewed holes in the box.
6. José took **pride** in his new bike.
7. Audrey lived in the **state** of Georgia.
8. Lucas said, "Those boots are **mine**."
9. A **dime** equals 10 cents.
10. Aaron was **done** with his piano lesson.
11. The rain fell on the window **pane**.
12. **Some** students go to school year round.
13. Landon rode his **bike** to school.
14. Justin didn't like the **stare** his sister gave him.
15. It is important to **care** for God's creation.

2 Choose the challenge word that best completes each sentence.
1. The students needed to **divide** their papers in half.
2. Mr. Tucker filled the car with **gasoline**.
3. Sophia learned to **whistle**.
4. A cat is a **feline**.
5. Mr. Riley was Mason's **uncle**.

Extended Activities:

1. Write the spelling words in alphabet cereal or pasta.

2. Ask students to choose two of the spelling words and draw pictures representing those words. Give an opportunity to share their pictures with the class.

3. Have students continue writing sentences for each spelling word in their notebooks.

4. Give students an opportunity to quiz each other on the spelling words and their definitions.

Lesson 154 – Apply Understanding of Words in Writing

Activities:

1. Give the students the page from the *Student Book* for this lesson. Students should also have their Bibles. If your students do not have KJV Bibles then prepare and duplicate the needed verses on a handout.

2. Read the directions for the activity sheet. You may wish to have students work together with a partner to complete the activity.

3. Complete the activity by having students read the Bible verses together. Students can take turns stating which vocabulary words they found in the verses.

Lesson 154   Name: _____

Look up the following Bible passages. After copying them, underline the spelling words that appear in the verses. Use the King James Version.

1. Matthew 6:9-13

Our Father which art in heaven. Hallowed be thy name. Thy kingdom come. Thy will be done in earth as it is in heaven. Give us this day our daily bread. And forgive us our debts, as we forgive our debtors. And lead us not into temptation but deliver us from evil: For thine is the kingdom, and the power, and the glory, for ever. Amen

2. I Peter 5:7

Casting all your care upon him; for He careth for you.

3. Joshua 24:15b

But as for me and my house, we will serve the LORD.

4. Proverbs 16:18

Pride goeth before destruction, and an haughty spirit before a fall.

5. John 10:14

I am the good shepherd, and know my sheep, and am known of mine.

246   Horizons Spelling Grade 3

Extended Activities:

1. Have students think of songs that include their spelling words.

2. Ask students to write each spelling word three times in three different colors.

3. Have the students continue writing sentences for each spelling word in their notebooks.

Lesson 155 – Assess and Evaluate Progress

Activities:

1. Give the students the page from the *Student Book* for this lesson. Tell the students that this is a "Check-up" page to see what they have learned during the week. (Note: Teachers/parents of home schoolers may decide what will be assessed. If a student does exceptionally well on the "What do you know?" pre-assessment, the teacher may choose not to test words already known by the student. Or the teacher may choose to test all words for the week.)

2. Tell students that you will say a word and use it in a sentence. They will listen to the word and the sentence. Then, they will write the word on the line next to the numbers. All challenge words are included in this review.

3. Say the word. Repeat it in the context of a sentence. Repeat the word.

4. The students write the dictated word.

5. The process is repeated until all words have been tested.

6. The teacher may correct in class by writing the words on the board and having the students compare or "self-correct" their work. The teacher may also correct each student's work individually.

7. The teacher then writes any corrections for words misspelled in the space provided.

8. The students study the misspelled words, and practice them on the second side of the Lesson page.

9. Space is provided for retesting, for testing additional sight or "challenge words" added for the week, and for additional practice.

Lesson 155 Name:

Check-up time!

Spelling Test

1.	13.
2.	14.
3.	15.
4.	16.
5.	17.
6.	18.
7.	19.
8.	20.
9.	21.
10.	22.
11.	23.
12.	24.

Corrections

Horizons Spelling Grade 3   247

Extended Activity:

Review any words missed. Send words to review home for additional study. Encourage all students in their efforts.

Week 32 - Skill Review

Lessons 156-160 — Once Again for Excellence

Goal: To review and study the spelling words from Lessons 121-155.

Review rules:
Review the rules for Weeks 25-31.

Teachers Note:
Students will review 28 words each day from the previous seven weeks. All of the words from the previous weeks will be reviewed. Students should know that only 28 words will appear on the final test, which are taken randomly from Weeks 25-31.

What Do You Remember?

Give the students the page from the *Student Book* for this lesson. Tell them that this page will be used to see what they currently know about the review. Ask them to listen carefully to each word as you say it, repeat it in a sentence, and say it once again. Follow the procedures for this page as described in the Introduction at the beginning of this *Teacher's Guide*.

Lessons 121-155
What do you remember?
Name: _____
Write the words your teacher reads.

1. partly
2. hasn't
3. wonder
4. hopped
5. myself
6. heal
7. yearly
8. I've
9. Sunday
10. rubbed
11. anything
12. lead
13. don't
14. careful
15. better
16. sinned
17. police officer
18. earth
19. sickness
20. deaf
21. yellow
22. bike
23. post office
24. wasn't
25. rinse
26. serve
27. state
28. flapped

249

Week 32 Worksheet Key

Week 32 Worksheet
Lessons 156-160
Name: _____

wonderful can't after stopped myself deaf forgetful
she's under lead rubbed crossword great happily
o'clock pretty pane tagged wallpaper kindly doesn't
funny planning state police officer leave pride rinse

1 Put the following groups of words in alphabetical order.

1. pride, pretty, rubbed, wonderful, kindly
kindly pretty pride rubbed wonderful

2. great, deaf, after, she's, under
after deaf great she's under

3. crossword, leave, myself, forgetful, happily
crossword forgetful happily leave myself

4. planning, doesn't, lead, pane, can't
can't doesn't lead pane planning

5. state, deaf, stopped, police officer, rinse
deaf police officer rinse state stopped

6. funny, o'clock, after, wallpaper, tagged
after funny o'clock tagged wallpaper

228

Lesson 156 – Practice Makes Perfect

Activities:

1. Give the students the page from the *Student Book* for this lesson.

2. Read to students the directions for the activity on the sheet.

3. After the students have completed the exercise, review the answers with the class.

4. You can extend the activity by having students write the leftover words on a sheet of paper.

Extended Activities for the Week:

1. Send a list of the spelling words from the previous seven weeks home for additional study. Remind parents and students that not all of the spelling words will appear on the final test. You may want to include a letter to the parents urging them to help the students both study and use the words from the previous seven weeks. Emphasize the importance of using spelling words in sentences, in speech, in stories, etc. so that they are given a context and not simply memorized.

2. Assign the reproducible *Week 32 Worksheet* either as homework or as an added classroom activity.

3. You may want to give spot quizzes to check student's spelling of the review words. Emphasize that these are not graded but are being used to help review.

Lesson 157 – Revisit for Success

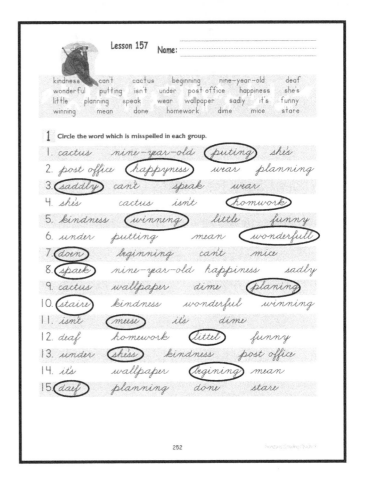

Activities:

1. Give the students the page from the *Student Book* for this lesson.

2. Review the words in the word box.

3. Read the directions with the students.

4. After they have completed the exercise, go over the correct answers.

5. You can extend the activity by having students write the misspelled words correctly on a sheet of paper.

Extended Activities:

1. Have students create word searches for 10 of the spelling words. They can then exchange their papers and find the spelling words in the word searches.

2. Ask students to write their spelling words both forward and backward.

3. You may want to give spot quizzes to check student's spelling of the review words. Emphasize that these are not graded but are being used to help review.

Lesson 158 – Become an Expert

Activities:

1. Give the students the page from the *Student Book* for this lesson.

2. Read the directions on the activity sheet with the students. Have them complete the top half of the activity sheet. When they have finished, review the answers as a class.

3. Have students complete the bottom half of the activity sheet. Point out that sentence #1 requires two words. Go over those answers as well.

Extended Activities:

1. Ask students to choose two of the spelling words and draw pictures representing those words. Give an opportunity to share their pictures with the class.

2. Have students write silly sentences using as many of the spelling words as they can.

3. Give students an opportunity to quiz each other on the spelling words and their definitions.

4. You may want to give spot quizzes to check student's spelling of the review words. Emphasize that these are not graded but are being used to help review.

Lesson 159 – Exercise for Mastery

Activities:

1. Give the students the page from the *Student Book* for this lesson.

2. Read the directions for the first activity on the sheet.

3. As a class, brainstorm silly, or not so silly sentences, using the spelling words.

4. Direct students in writing their own sentences.

Extended Activities:

1. Share sentences.

2. Write silly sentences using other of the review spelling words.

3. You may want to give spot quizzes to check student's spelling of the review words. Emphasize that these are not graded but are being used to help review.

Lesson 160 – Assess and Evaluate

Activities:

1. Give the students the page from the *Student Book* for this lesson. Tell the students that this is a "Check-up" page to see what they have learned during the week.

2. Tell students that you will say a word and use it in a sentence. They will listen to the word and the sentence. Then, they will write the word on the line next to the numbers.

3. Say the word. Repeat it in the context of a sentence. Repeat the word.

4. The students write the dictated word.

5. The process is repeated until all words have been tested.

6. The teacher may correct in class by writing the words on the board and having the students compare or "self-correct" their work. The teacher may also correct each student's work individually.

7. The teacher then writes any corrections for words misspelled in the space provided.

8. The students study the misspelled words, and practice them on the second side of the Lesson page.

9. Space is provided for retesting, and for additional practice.

Test:

happiness	I'd	letter	dragged
bedroom	peach	sickly	you'd
apple	swimming	good-bye	speak
sadness	don't	Sunday	bike
putting	family tree	kindness	earth
done	they're	stare	wonder
getting	butterfly	learn	serve

Extended Activity:

Review any words missed. Send words to review home for additional study. Encourage all students in their efforts.

Reproducible Practice Pages

Week 1 Worksheet
Lessons 1-5

Name: _____

class	clean	clip	close	broke	bring	brown
brush	cloth	draw	drink	drive	from	friend	front

1 Find each spelling word in the word search. Write the words on the lines below.

```
C S B V I D E H F F D
P L R F R G B T R Z N
N Z O Y R R V O C X E
C H K S I O K L T S I
L B E N E N N C C D R
I V G G I H P T R L F
P E G R S P S A S Z J
Z O D S N V W U X E O
G F A C L E A N R R B
W L D R I V E D V B B
C N W O R B M O R F R
```

Name: _____

1 Fill in the blank with the blend or diagraph that fits each word. The blends and
diagraphs for this lesson are *th, ch, rd,* and *sh.*

mu____   ____e   ____is

____ild   bi____   ____ey

toge____er   sear____   ba____

wo____   cat____   di____

____eep   ____all   ____ink

Week 3 Worksheet
Lessons 11-15

Name: _____

1   **Circle the word in each row that is spelled correctly.**

waerm	warme	warm
heur	her	herr
starte	staert	start
fir	firr	foir
storme	stoerm	storm
far	faer	farr
never	navre	neuvre
harde	haerd	hard
werre	were	weure
color	coler	couler
caer	car	carr
turn	terne	turne
woern	woorn	worn
yarde	yeard	yard
work	woerk	worke

Week 4 Worksheet
Lessons 16-20

Name: _____

1 Use each set of words in a sentence.

man   hat   today

_____

stand   last   always

_____

face   and   may

_____

always   along   map

_____

2 Use these words to write other sentences.

day   ask   than   Monday   crayon   camping   trail   holiday

_____

_____

_____

_____

Horizons Spelling Grade 3

Week 5 Worksheet
Lessons 21-25

Name: _____

best	read	be	only	many	freed	then	agree
see	these	very	every	Jesus	spell	family

1 Choose the spelling word that is the opposite or antonym of the given word.

all _____

jailed _____

few _____

blind _____

worst _____

disagree _____

single one _____

2 Choose the spelling word that is the same or synonym of the given word.

Christ _____

all _____

greatly _____

live _____

later _____

household _____

understand _____

write _____

Wednesday   feather   breakfast   instead   behind

3 Copy the challenge words.

_____

_____

Week 6 Worksheet
Lessons 26-30

Name:

if   his   pick   like   big   find   white   with   might   my   why
giving   wish   sing   eyes   American   recycle   lightning   winter   visit

1 Fill in the blank with the word that fits the clue and put the words in a crossword puzzle. Not all spelling words will be used.

Puzzle 1

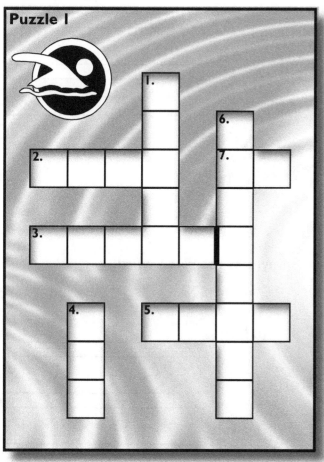

Puzzle 2

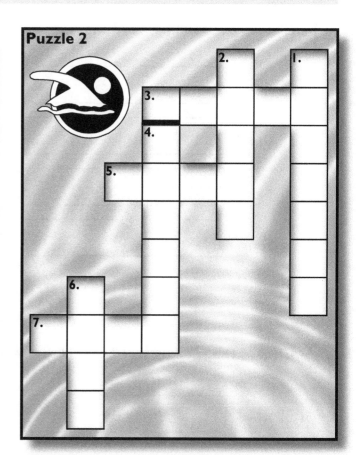

5a. April helps her mom _____ beans.

4d. A bear is a very _____ animal.

7a. _____ bike is the red one.

2a. Harrison has green _____.

6d. An _____ flag flew over the court house.

3a. _____ is a cold time of year.

1d. Brook went to _____ her grandmother.

6d. Mrs. Light could not _____ her car keys.

3a. The color of snow is _____.

2d. Madison and Mark _____ go to the park.

4d. Mrs. Simons is _____ her daughter a haircut.

7a. Jenny likes to _____ "Jesus Loves Me."

1d. A newspaper is something that many people _____.

5a. Angela made a birthday _____

Horizons Spelling Grade 3

Week 7 Worksheet
Lessons 31-35

Name:

grow	long	old	open	those	hot	both	goes	most	coat	soak
God	ago	owner	roll	Jehovah	volleyball	orange	toast	collar		

1 **Underline the correct word to complete each sentence.**

1. Jason **goes/ago** to soccer practice on Tuesday.

2. Grace wore her **coat/roll** to school.

3. The door was left **long/open** after recess.

4. Kim needed to be careful of the **hot/owner** stove.

5. **Both/Those** of the girls wanted pizza for lunch.

6. Maria plans to **grow/soak** beans in her garden.

2 **Underline the correct challenge word to complete each sentence.**

1. Malory enjoyed playing **collar/volleyball** at recess.

2. David ate an **orange/toast** for breakfast.

Week 8 Worksheet
Lessons 36-40

stand	goes	both	hot	grow	sing	white
every	read	then	only	be	along	ask
broke	bring	from	friend	front	word	dish
hard	car	were	map	man	than	may

1 Arrange the following words in alphabetical order.

stand read from map _____

only hard goes then _____

be sing ask along _____

dish word man may _____

2 Circle the word that is spelled correctly in each row. At the bottom of the page correctly write the words that are misspelled.

everey	brinng	were
freind	brocke	car
hott	both	grouw
white	frount	thane

_____

_____

_____

Horizons Spelling Grade 3

Week 9 Worksheet
Lessons 41-45

Name: _____

small	ball	call	because	walk	straw	chalk
sauce	naughty	paws	tall	water	wash	talk	law

1 Fill in the blank with the correct spelling word.

1. Kyle likes to use a _____ when he drinks lemonade.
2. Holly and Megan _____ their hands before lunch.
3. The students made _____ drawings in art class.
4. The students had indoor recess _____ it was raining outside.
5. Clark asked for a glass of _____.
6. Mrs. Ritter will _____ the dentist for an appointment.
7. Spaghetti _____ is made from tomatoes.
8. Stephan and Andre _____ their dog after school.
9. The _____ child needed to leave the party.
10. The water tower was very _____.
11. Julian ate a _____ bowl of ice cream before going to bed.
12. The dog had dirty _____.
13. Rosa can _____ to her grandma on the phone every week.
14. Kirsten liked the pink and orange soccer _____ she received for her birthday.
15. Police officers make sure people follow the _____.

2 Challenge Words

basketball   macaw   Utah   laundry   faucet

1. Jeremy plays _____ with his brothers.
2. The leaky _____ needed to be fixed.
3. The capital of _____ is Salt Lake City.
4. A _____ is a beautiful bird found in the rain forest.
5. Olivia helps her mom do _____.

Week 10 Worksheet
Lessons 46-50

Name: _____

1 **Underline the correct word for each sentence.**

1. Mr. Carson made a camp **fire/dive** for his family.

2. Jonah asked if he could **name/take** his dog for a walk.

3. Mrs. Hobart **make/made** a pumpkin pie last week.

4. The bee **home/hive** was a busy place.

5. Elliot asked for **more/fine** ice cream.

6. The mail **came/before** early yesterday.

2 **Underline the correct challenge word for each sentence.**

1. The caterpillar **grade/became** a butterfly.

2. Mrs. Foster planned to **bathe/surprise** her infant and wash her hair.

Horizons Spelling Grade 3

Week 11 Worksheet
Lessons 51-55

Name: _____

| jumping | showing | hunting | falling | holding | helping | playing |
| riding | pulling | thanking | using | leaving | ending | hiding | hurting |

Challenge Words   pleasing   bicycling   drying   flying   numbering

1 **Fill in the blank with the correct spelling word.**

1. Paul liked books with a happy _____.
2. The _____ rain kept Patrick from playing outside.
3. Mr. Kim was _____ for the airport on Monday.
4. Tyson found the mice _____ under the bed.
5. The squirrel was _____ acorns.
6. The cook was _____ a hot pan.
7. The movie was _____ at seven p.m.
8. Mrs. Lancer was _____ her class for the birthday gift.
9. Keaton's arm was _____ after the flu shot.
10. Kerry liked _____ horses.
11. The frog was _____ into the pond.
12. Madison enjoyed _____ others.
13. The children were _____ the game outside.
14. Angie was _____ her sister's coat.
15. The mother was _____ her child in a wagon.

2 **Fill in the blank with the correct challenge word.**

1. The smell of apple blossoms is _____.
2. The birds were _____ south for the winter.
3. Erica went _____ with her friend.
4. Mrs. Steward was _____ her clothes outside.
5. Jason was _____ his spelling list.

Week 12 Worksheet
Lessons 56-60

Name: _____

girls   boxes   hands   tells   beds   hopes   loves   dresses   sixes   washes   itches
tries   flies   foxes   toys   batteries   Christians   Bibles   churches   marches

1 The vowels are missing in the following words. Write the words correctly with the vowels.

1. grls _____

2. tlls _____

3. lvs _____

4. wshs _____

5. fls _____

6. bxs _____

7. bds _____

8. drsss _____

9. tchs _____

10. fxs _____

11. hnds _____

12. hps _____

13. sxs _____

14. trs _____

15. tys _____

2 The vowels are missing in the challenge words.
Write the words correctly on the blanks.

1. mrchs _____

2. Bbls _____

3. bttrs _____

4. chrchs _____

5. Chrstns _____

208

Week 13 Worksheet
Lessons 61-65

1 Each spelling word is written backward. Write the words forward.

1. eerht _____

2. thgie _____

3. driht _____

4. ruof _____

5. enin _____

6. dnoces _____

7. orez _____

8. net _____

9. evif _____

10. owt _____

11. neves _____

12. eno _____

13. tsrif _____

14. htruof _____

15. xis _____

2 Each challenge word is written backward. Write the words forward.

1. nevele _____

2. ytnewt _____

3. derdnuh eno _____

4. evlewt _____

5. neetriht _____

Week 14 Worksheet
Lessons 66-70

Name: _____

by   buy   new   knew   their   there   they're   no   know   here   hear

pair   pear   so   sew   **Challenge Words**   dear   deer   aisle   isle   I'll

1 **Write the spelling word that goes with each picture.**

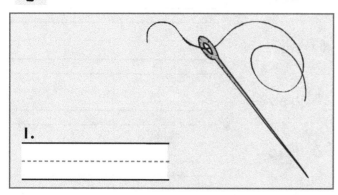

1. _____

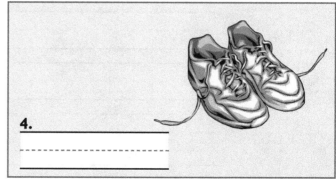

4. _____

2. _____

5. _____

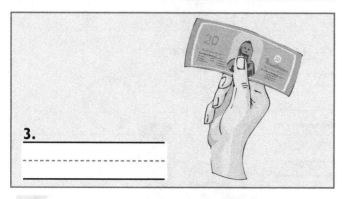

3. _____

2 **Write the challenge word that goes with each picture.**

1. _____

2. _____

Week 15 Worksheet
Lessons 71-75

Name: _____

hour	our	in	inn	blue	blew	ant
aunt	hole	whole	son	sun	or	oar	ore

1 Choose the spelling word which fits each clue. Not all of the spelling words will be used.

Across
2 this shines in the sky
3 a place to stay at night
6 something missing from the center of a donut
7 the entire thing
9 not out but

Down
1 a small animal
2 a male child
4 a strong wind has done this
5 the color of the sky
6 one of 24 in a day
8 something used to move a boat

Week 16 Worksheet
Lessons 76-80

small	jumping	falling	by	blue	ball	fire
three	seven	or	laws	bed	ten	ore
second	ending	talk	inn	paws	fine	zero
boxes	naughty	showing	helping	water	tall	hour

1 **Choose the word used incorrectly in each group.**

1. ☐ a. the book's **ending** was exciting
   b. a **secund** helping
   c. an **hour** a day
   d. an extra **helping** of potatoes

2. ☐ a. a **tall** tree
   b. packing the **boxes**
   c. **helping** her mother
   d. a **naughtey** puppy

3. ☐ a. **showeing** a house
   b. **zero** problems wrong
   c. **jumping** jacks
   d. iron **ore**

4. ☐ a. dog's **pawes**
   b. coal **ore**
   c. **small** helping
   d. **three** friends

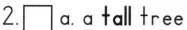

5. ☐ a. an **our** long
   b. traffic **law**
   c. **fire** engine
   d. an **ending** note

6. ☐ a. **blue** sky
   b. a **tall** building
   c. **second** grade
   d. **falleng** water

7. ☐ a. **water** fountain
   b. **sefen**-years-old
   c. **ten** toes
   d. a **fine** day

8. ☐ a. **showing** a painting
   b. **zero** answers wrong
   c. the cat's **paws**
   d. **buy** a river

9. ☐ a. **fine** hair
   b. a **ball** park
   c. **talck** to the teacher
   d. staying at an **inn**

10. ☐ a. a bunk **bed**
    b. either a bike **our** a kite
    c. a **ball** game
    d. **by** tomorrow morning

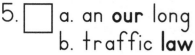

Week 17 Worksheet
Lessons 81-85

1 If the spelling word is used and spelled correctly, write **C** for correct. If the spelling word is used or spelled wrong, write **W** for wrong.

1. The <u>duk</u> quacked. _____
2. Nicole hurt her <u>thumb</u>. _____
3. The <u>lam</u> had white wool. _____
4. Squirrels are <u>quicke</u> runners. _____
5. Bridgett had a band-aid on her <u>knee</u>. _____
6. Nathan needed to <u>right</u> his name on the paper. _____
7. Everyone was <u>queit</u> during the pastor's sermon. _____
8. Mr. Waylon took a <u>wrong</u> turn. _____
9. The <u>black</u> bird sat in a tree. _____
10. There was a <u>crak</u> in the cement. _____
11. Jake planned to <u>wrap</u> his sister's gift. _____
12. Bella needed to <u>combe</u> her hair. _____
13. Mrs. Ray used a <u>nife</u> to cut her steak. _____
14. Ben and Jordan like to <u>climb</u> trees. _____
15. The child did not like the sound of the pig's <u>squeal</u>. _____

2 If the challenge word is used and spelled correctly, write **C** for correct. If the challenge word is used or spelled wrong, write **W** for wrong.

1. Brenda had <u>knowledge</u> of all fifty states. _____
2. The <u>honeycome</u> was hidden in the woods. _____
3. Josh played <u>tackle</u> football with his friends. _____
4. The <u>chicken</u> drove the car. _____
5. Hope ate <u>crackers</u> with peanut butter. _____

Week 18 Worksheet
Lessons 86-90

Word Bank: about   down   how   house
point   boy   around   oil

1 **Choose the spelling word that rhymes with the listed word.**

1. mouse _____

2. shout _____

3. bound _____

4. frown _____

5. anoint _____

6. now _____

7. joy _____

8. spoil _____

Word Bank: enjoy   royal   found   ground
toy   now   round

2 **Choose the spelling word that is the opposite of the given word.**

1. weapon _____

2. lost _____

3. hate _____

4. later _____

5. sky _____

6. square _____

7. regular _____

Week 19 Worksheet
Lessons 91-95

1 **Fill in the blank with the missing j or s sound to complete the spelling word.**

1. __unk
2. __ircle
3. __avior
4. pre__s
5. a__e
6. lar__e
7. __ump
8. __in
9. __it
10. __in__e
11. __ity
12. __ym
13. pa__e
14. garba__e
15. __enter

2 **Fill in the blank with the missing j or s sound to complete the challenge word.**

1. bad__e
2. __ourney
3. ve__etables
4. ca__tle
5. __anuary

Week 20 Worksheet
Lessons 96-100

keep	bee	green	sleep	tree	bleed	deep
look	good	soon	school	book	food	took	foot

1 Find the spelling words in the word search. **When you have found a word, write it on a line below the word search.**

```
V B B L U B S Z A E H Q
F O N B F X Y F P P C D
F U L O B H M B D B A D
B O O C L L N J H Z L O
F T O Z K O E O J K T U
D W H D O O N E E E B N
O L C S P E O E D E O T
O M S E E N O L N P I O
G S G R C S T B O O K O
D I G B S R C Z K N C K
X E V L E D Z L F N A B
J S L E E P E E D G M T
```

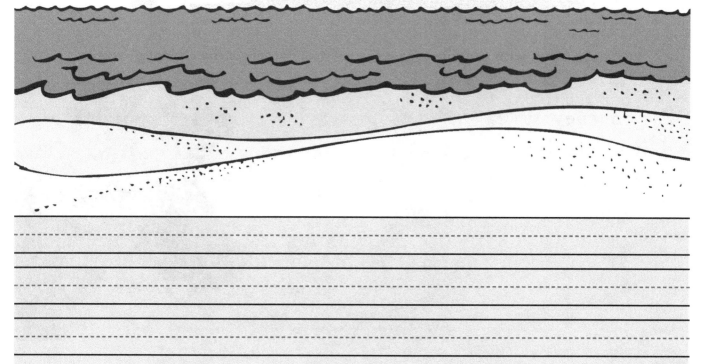

Horizons Spelling Grade 3

Week 21 Worksheet
Lessons 101-105

Name: _____

1 **Put the spelling words in alphabetical order.**

1. light, enough, bought, ghastly, brought

_____

_____

2. ghetto, laugh, rough, though, taught

_____

_____

3. ghost, night, through, fight, tough

_____

_____

2 **Put the challenge words in alphabetical order.**

straight, delight, laughter, cough, spaghetti

_____

_____

_____

Week 22 Worksheet
Lessons 106-110

1 Put an **X** in the box of the phrase where the spelling word is used correctly.

1. a. I have go
   b. I go
   c. I have went
   d. I gone

2. a. He do homework
   b. They had did homework
   c. She has do homework
   d. He does homework

3. a. Yesterday he ran
   b. Yesterday he run
   c. She will ran
   d. He run fast

4. a. She had give
   b. He will ate
   c. They gave
   d. They had eat

5. a. They will has
   b. She has
   c. He have
   d. They will had

6. a. He went
   b. She go
   c. He gone to the store
   d. She go yesterday

7. a. She will ran
   b. They have eat
   c. He ate
   d. She run

8. a. They does
   b. He did yesterday
   c. He will does
   d. He do tomorrow

9. a. She will gave
   b. He had give
   c. They will give
   d. She will have give

2 Put an **X** in the box of the phrase where the challenge word is used correctly.

1. a. He see
   b. They saw
   c. She will seen
   d. He will saw

2. a. She will said
   b. He had say
   c. She said
   d. They will said

Week 23 Worksheet
Lessons 111-115

unjust   unsafe   unhappy   unwrap   reopen   replay   refill
disagree   discolored   disorder   dislike   preview   prefix   prepare
present   discontinue   prevent   repent   unrepentant   return

1 Fill in the blank with the correct spelling word.

1. Cassandra couldn't wait to _____ her birthday present.
2. The room was in _____ after the party.
3. Melody was _____ with her new haircut.
4. Brandon asked for a _____ on his milk.
5. The old bridge looked _____.
6. The store planned to _____ on Friday.
7. Mr. Pullman planned to _____ supper at 5:00 p.m.
8. The mayor will _____ the award.
9. The sunlight _____ the curtains.
10. An example of a _____ is un.
11. The movie _____ looked exciting.
12. Grant and Wyatt _____ dusting their rooms.
13. The child thought his punishment was _____.
14. The referee asked the team to _____ the point.
15. The students _____ as to which game to play at recess.

2 Fill in the blank with the correct challenge word.

1. The store planned to _____ selling candy.
2. Sunscreen helps _____ sunburn.
3. The mean young person was _____ of his sins.
4. The mean young person needed to _____ of his sins.
5. Mrs. James needs to _____ a pair of shoes.

Week 24 Worksheet
Lessons 116-120

Name: _____

comb climb knee write how around royal wrong boy enjoy
gym large junk garbage Savior since book foot tree ghetto
though give reopen went unsafe has disorder preview

1 Find each word in the word search. Write the words on the lines below.

```
W U G M R E D R O S I D
E E Y H L T D R H A S G
I G G A E N R T V I I K
V W Y A U T R E N V O L
E O O O B E T C E O T A
R B R H O R E O B N H R
P A M P E F A S N U O G
T G E I E S G Y E U E
T N E W L N N E O T G K
W R O N G C J K B I H N
F O O T G B M O C R V U
S A V I O R Z M Y W F J
```

_____
_____
_____
_____
_____
_____
_____
_____

Week 25 Worksheet
Lessons 121-125

kindly   kindness   fully   partly   yearly   careful   carefully
wonderful   forgetful   happily   happiness   sickly   sickness
sadness   sadly   beautiful   lonely   loneliness   joyful   joyfulness

1 **Add ly to the following words.**

kind _____

full _____

part _____

year _____

happy _____

sick _____

sad _____

careful _____

2 **Add ful to the following words.**

care _____

wonder _____

forget _____

3 **Add ness to the following words.**

sad _____

sick _____

happy _____

kind _____

4 **Write the challenge words.**

_____

_____

_____

_____

_____

_____

_____

Week 26 Worksheet
Lessons 126-130

Name: _____

can't   isn't   she's   o'clock   I'd   you'd   hasn't
I've   don't   didn't   doesn't   they're   it's   wasn't
we'll   couldn't   shouldn't   you're   won't   haven't

2 Make the following spelling words into contractions.

1. she is _____

2. was not _____

3. has not _____

4. did not _____

5. can not _____

6. I would _____

7. do not _____

8. of the clock _____

9. it is _____

10. you would _____

11. they are _____

12. is not _____

13. we will _____

14. does not _____

15. I have _____

2 Make the following challenge words into contractions.

1. you are _____

2. have not _____

3. could not _____

4. will not _____

5. should not _____

Week 27 Worksheet
Lessons 131-135

Name: _____

sister	after	cactus	under	order	monkey	wonder
Sunday	better	yellow	apple	letter	little	funny
pretty	yesterday	Tuesday	rabbit	balloon	marble	

1 **Add vowels to the following letters to form the spelling words.**

1. wndr _____

2. lttr _____

3. bttr _____

4. rdr _____

5. prtty _____

6. ftr _____

7. Sndy _____

8. ppl _____

9. lttl _____

10. ccts _____

11. sstr _____

12. yllw _____

13. ndr _____

14. mnky _____

15. fnny _____

2 **Add vowels to the following letters to form the challenge words.**

1. Tsdy _____

2. blln _____

3. ystrdy _____

4. mrbl _____

5. rbbt _____

stopped   dragged   hopped   rubbed   sinned   tagged   topped   swimming
beginning   putting   running   planning   winning   getting   flapped

1 Choose the spelling word which fits each clue. Not all of the spelling words will be used.

ACROSS
- 2 To finish first
- 4 Move against
- 6 Not able to go any more
- 8 Preparing
- 9 At the start
- 10 To be brought behind
- 12 Put above
- 13 To go against God's word

DOWN
- 1 You're it
- 3 Jump up and down
- 4 Moving fast on a track
- 5 Birds do this
- 6 To move through the pool
- 7 Placing
- 11 Receiving

224

Week 29 Worksheet
Lessons 141-145

Name: _____

myself anything crossword bedroom butterfly homework wallpaper grandparents
sister-in-law good-bye nine-year-old post office good-looking family-tree police officer
challenge words childlike washing machine handkerchief stagecoach best-selling

1 **List the spelling words which are hyphenated compounds.**

_____
_____
_____

2 **List the spelling words which are open compounds.**

_____
_____
_____

3 **List the spelling words which are closed compounds.**

_____
_____
_____
_____

4 **List the challenge words which are hyphenated compounds.**

_____

5 **List the challenge words which are open compounds.**

_____

6 **List the challenge words which are closed compounds.**

_____
_____

beat	deaf	great	heal	lead	peach	leave
speak	wear	early	earth	learn	mean	real	reason

1 **Find each spelling word in the word search. Write the words on the lines below.**

```
I B J R U P H I C G
P R E L E T Z D J R
Y X A A R A C S I E
L E C A T D S H M A
R H E L R E E O W T
A K K L E A R N N J
E D X A L F E G N P
C Q R W E U C W A K
E V A E L P J I E Y
V D A E L A S Q M O
```

Week 31 Worksheet
Lessons 151-155

done   come   some   bite   care   dime   mice   mine   state   stare   pane
pride   rinse   serve   bike   whistle   uncle   feline   gasoline   divide

1   **Underline the misspelled word in each sentence. Write the word correctly.**

1. Victoria rode her bike with peride. _____

2. Mrs. Hunter washed and rinsed the pain of glass. _____

3. Mr. Walker said he was doun with supper and couldn't eat one
   more bite. _____

4. Mrs. Penn was not happy to find some meece in
   her home. _____

5. Ryan said, "That dime is minne. _____

6. Logan planned to seurve his family their meal. _____

7. Ella planned to cume to Hannah's birthday party. _____

8. Noah planned to take good caere of his new bike. _____

9. Elijah stared at the staet map. _____

2   **Underline the misspelled challenge word in each sentence. Write the word correctly.**

1. Tony's uncle taught him to wistle. _____

2. Mrs. Marshall planned to devide the last piece of
   pizza in half. _____

3. The felline did not like the smell of gasoline. _____

Week 32 Worksheet
Lessons 156-160

Name: _____

wonderful   can't   after   stopped   myself   deaf   forgetful
she's   under   lead   rubbed   crossword   great   happily
o'clock   pretty   pane   tagged   wallpaper   kindly   doesn't
funny   planning   state   police officer   leave   pride   rinse

1 **Put the following groups of words in alphabetical order.**

1. pride, pretty, rubbed, wonderful, kindly

2. great, deaf, after, she's, under

3. crossword, leave, myself, forgetful, happily

4. planning, doesn't, lead, pane, can't

5. state, deaf, stopped, police officer, rinse

6. funny, o' clock, after, wallpaper, tagged

Word Lists

Horizons Spelling 3
Word List

Week 1	Week 2	Week 3	Week 4
Spelling Words	**Spelling Words**	**Spelling Words**	**Spelling Words**
class	the	warm	and
clean	this	start	always
clip	think	fir	day
close	they	her	today
broke	together	color	face
bring	bath	turn	ask
brown	word	far	hat
brush	bird	never	last
cloth	much	hard	map
draw	search	car	away
drink	catch	work	man
drive	child	yard	than
from	dish	worn	may
friend	sheep	were	along
front	shall	storm	stand
Challenge Words	**Challenge Words**	**Challenge Words**	**Challenge Words**
clown	Thursday	turkey	Monday
broom	father	acorn	crayon
drawer	heard	afternoon	camping
Friday	shepherd	finger	trail
afraid	shoe	Saturday	holiday

Horizons Spelling 3
Word List

Week 5	Week 6	Week 7	Week 8
Spelling Words	**Spelling Words**	**Spelling Words**	
best	if	grow	Review all
read	his	long	Spelling Words
be	pick	old	Weeks 1-7
only	like	open	
many	big	those	
freed	find	hot	
then	white	both	
agree	with	goes	
see	might	most	
these	my	coat	
very	why	soak	
every	giving	God	
Jesus	wish	ago	
spell	sing	owner	
family	eyes	roll	
Challenge Words	**Challenge Words**	**Challenge Words**	
Wednesday	American	Jehovah	
feather	recycle	volleyball	
breakfast	lightning	orange	
instead	winter	toast	
behind	visit	collar	

Horizons Spelling 3
Word List

Week 9	Week 10	Week 11	Week 12
Spelling Words	**Spelling Words**	**Spelling Words**	**Spelling Words**
small	make	jumping	girls
ball	take	showing	boxes
call	came	hunting	hands
because	hive	falling	tells
walk	made	holding	beds
sauce	more	helping	hopes
straw	name	playing	loves
chalk	fine	riding	dresses
naughty	same	pulling	sixes
paws	fire	thanking	washes
tall	before	using	itches
water	home	leaving	tries
wash	cute	ending	flies
talk	dive	hiding	foxes
law	live	hurting	toys
Challenge Words	**Challenge Words**	**Challenge Words**	**Challenge Words**
basketball	grade	pleasing	batteries
macaw	became	bicycling	Christians
Utah	bathe	drying	Bibles
laundry	surprise	flying	churches
faucet	cube	numbering	marches

Horizons Spelling 3
Word List

Week 13

Spelling Words
zero
one
two
three
four
five
six
seven
eight
nine
ten
first
second
third
fourth

Challenge Words
eleven
twelve
thirteen
twenty
one hundred

Week 14

Spelling Words
by
buy
new
knew
their
there
they're
no
know
here
hear
pair
pear
so
sew

Challenge Words
dear
deer
aisle
isle
I'll

Week 15

Spelling Words
hour
our
in
inn
blue
blew
ant
aunt
hole
whole
son
sun
or
oar
ore

Challenge Words
flour
flower
way
weigh
homonym

Week 16

Review all
Spelling Words
Weeks 9-15

Horizons Spelling 3
Word List

Week 17	Week 18	Week 19	Week 20
Spelling Words	Spelling Words	Spelling Words	Spelling Words
comb	about	city	keep
knife	boy	age	bee
knee	enjoy	Savior	green
write	toy	sin	sleep
wrong	royal	page	tree
wrap	down	press	bleed
black	how	large	deep
crack	now	garbage	look
duck	around	sit	good
climb	house	center	soon
lamb	found	gym	school
thumb	round	jump	book
quick	ground	circle	food
squeal	oil	junk	took
quiet	point	since	foot
Challenge Words	Challenge Words	Challenge Words	Challenge Words
tackle	tower	vegetables	cheese
chicken	choice	journey	cookie
knowledge	rejoice	castle	shook
crackers	wound	January	creep
honeycomb	employment	badge	goose

Horizons Spelling 3
Word List

Week 21

Spelling Words
light
ghetto
ghost
night
through
laugh
rough
enough
bought
ghastly
though
fight
brought
taught
tough

Challenge Words
laughter
straight
spaghetti
cough
delight

Week 22

Spelling Words
go
went
gone
run
ran
did
do
does
eat
ate
had
has
have
gave
give

Challenge Words
saw
see
seen
say
said

Week 23

Spelling Words
unjust
unsafe
unhappy
unwrap
reopen
replay
refill
disagree
discolored
disorder
dislike
preview
prefix
prepare
present

Challenge Words
prevent
repent
return
discontinue
unrepentant

Week 24

Review all
Spelling Words
Weeks 17–23

Horizons Spelling 3
Word List

Week 25	Week 26	Week 27	Week 28
Spelling Words	Spelling Words	Spelling Words	Spelling Words
kindly	can't	sister	stopped
kindness	isn't	after	dragged
fully	she's	cactus	hopped
partly	o'clock	under	rubbed
yearly	I'd	order	sinned
careful	you'd	monkey	tagged
carefully	hasn't	wonder	topped
wonderful	I've	Sunday	swimming
forgetful	don't	better	beginning
happily	didn't	yellow	putting
happiness	doesn't	apple	running
sickly	they're	letter	planning
sickness	it's	little	winning
sadness	wasn't	funny	getting
sadly	we'll	pretty	flapped
Challenge Words	Challenge Words	Challenge Words	Challenge Words
beautiful	couldn't	yesterday	admitted
lonely	shouldn't	Tuesday	permitted
loneliness	you're	rabbit	referring
joyful	won't	balloon	skipping
joyfulness	haven't	marble	slipped

Horizons Spelling 3
Word List

Week 29

Spelling Words
myself
anything
crossword
bedroom
butterfly
homework
wallpaper
grandparents
sister-in-law
good-bye
nine-year-old
post office
good-looking
family-tree
police officer

Challenge Words
childlike
washing machine
handkerchief
stagecoach
best-selling

Week 30

Spelling Words
beat
deaf
great
heal
lead
peach
leave
speak
wear
early
earth
learn
mean
real
reason

Challenge Words
creation
heaven
measure
season
weapon

Week 31

Spelling Words
done
come
some
bite
care
dime
mice
mine
state
stare
pane
pride
rinse
serve
bike

Challenge Words
whistle
uncle
feline
gasoline
divide

Week 32

Review all
Spelling Words
Weeks 25-31

Horizons Spelling Grades 1-3
Cumulative Word List

A

a	afraid	airport	American	April	August
about	after	aisle	an	are	aunt
ache	afternoon	all	and	arm	away
acorn	age	along	ant	around	ax
across	ago	alphabet	anyone	ask	axes
add	agree	always	anything	asked	
admitted	airplane	am	apple	ate	

B

baby	beautiful	bell	bird	book	broke
back	became	below	birthday	books	broom
badge	because	belt	bite	boot	brother
ball	become	beside	bitter	both	brought
balloon	bed	best	black	bottle	brown
bare	bedroom	best-selling	blame	bought	brush
baseball	beds	better	bleed	bowl	bubble
basketball	bee	between	blend	box	burn
bath	been	beyond	bless	boxes	but
bathe	bees	Bibles	blew	boy	butter
batter	before	bicycling	blow	boy's	butterfly
batteries	began	big	blue	brave	buy
be	begging	bigger	bluff	bread	by
beaches	beginning	biggest	boat	break	
bear	behind	bike	boil	breakfast	
beat	believe	bind	bone	bring	

Horizons Spelling Grades 1-3
Cumulative Word List (Cont.)

C

cactus	castle	chill	class	cold	crack
cage	cat	chime	classes	collar	crackers
call	catch	chin	clay	color	crayon
called	cattle	choice	clean	comb	creation
calling	cent	Christ	click	come	creep
came	center	Christian	climb	cook	cross
camping	chalk	Christians	clip	cooked	crossword
can	cheese	Christmas	clock	cookie	cry
can't	chick	church	close	cool	cube
cape	chicken	churches	cloth	cooled	cuff
car	child	circle	clothes	cot	cupful
care	childlike	circus	cloud	cough	curb
careful	children	city	clown	could	cut
carefully	children's	clang	coat	couldn't	cute
careless	child's	clasp	cob	count	

D

daddy	delight	discolored	divide	don't	dresses
day	did	discontinue	do	door	drink
deaf	didn't	dish	dock	down	drive
dear	dime	dishes	does	dragged	drop
December	dinner	dislike	doesn't	draw	drying
deep	dirt	disorder	dolls	drawer	duck
deer	disagree	dive	done	dream	

E

each	echo	eighty	ending	entire
early	eggs	elephant	enjoy	entrust
earth	eight	eleven	enjoyment	every
Easter	eighteen	employment	enlarge	eye
eat	eighth	enclose	enough	eyes

F

face	feather	fir	flour	forgot	Friday
falling	February	fire	flower	forty	friend
family	feet	first	fly	found	friendship
family tree	feline	five	flying	four	fries
far	fifteen	fix	foam	fourteen	frog
farm	fifth	flake	food	fourth	from
faster	fifty	flame	foot	fox	front
fastest	fight	flapped	football	foxes	fully
father	find	flew	for	foxhole	funny
faucet	fine	flies	forget	free	fur
fearless	finger	float	forgetful	freed	

G

garbage	ghastly	girls	gnaw	good-looking	ground
gas	ghetto	give	gnome	goodness	grow
gasoline	ghost	giving	go	goose	guess
gate	giant	glad	goat	gopher	gum
gave	gift	glass	God	grade	gym
geese	giggle	globe	goes	grandparents	
gentle	ginger	glue	gone	grateful	
get	girl	gnash	good	great	
getting	girl's	gnat	good-bye	green	

H

had	has	heard	higher	honeycomb	houses
hammer	hasn't	heaven	highest	hood	how
handful	hat	helpful	hiked	hop	huddle
handkerchief	have	helping	him	hope	huge
hands	haven't	helpless	his	hopeless	hugged
hang	he	hem	hive	hopes	hugging
happier	he'd	her	holding	hoping	hundred
happiest	he'll	here	hole	hopped	hunting
happily	head	hers	holiday	hopping	hurting
happiness	headache	hide	home	hot	
happy	heal	hiding	homework	hour	
hard	hear	high	homonym	house	

Horizons Spelling Grades 1-3
Cumulative Word List (Cont.)

I

I	if	in	instead	it	its
ice	I'll	inn	isle	itch	it's
I'd	I'm	inside	isn't	itches	I've

J

January	join	joy	judgement	jump	junk
Jehovah	joke	joyful	juggle	jumping	just
Jesus	journey	joyfulness	July	June	

K

keep	kindest	kneads	knew	knock	known
kettle	kindly	knee	knife	knot	knows
kind	kindness	kneel	knight	know	
kinder	kites	knees	knives	knowledge	

Horizons Spelling Grades 1-3
Cumulative Word List (Cont.)

L

lad	laughter	lemon	lip	loneliness	love
ladder	laundry	less	little	lonely	loves
lamb	law	letter	littler	long	low
large	lead	lick	littlest	longer	luck
lass	learn	life	live	longest	lunch
last	leave	light	lives	look	lunches
latch	leaving	lightning	loaded	looked	lung
laugh	leg	like	lock	looking	

M

macaw	March	measure	middle	mommy	mother
made	marches	meat	might	Monday	mouth
mail	match	meatloaf	mile	monkey	Mr.
mailman	math	meek	mine	moon	Mrs.
make	may	meet	miss	moonlight	much
man	May	melted	mix	mop	must
many	me	men	mixed	more	my
map	meal	met	mixes	morning	myself
marble	mean	mice	mom	most	

N

name	never	night	nine-year-old	noise	November
naughty	new	nine	ninth	noon	now
needs	nibble	nineteen	no	nose	nowhere
nerve	nice	ninety	nod	not	numbering
					nurse

O

oar	oil	one hundred	orange	our	owner
o'clock	old	only	order	out	ox
October	on	open	ore	outside	oxen
off	one	or	other	over	

P

pack	paws	pets	plant	pond	prevent
paddle	peace	phone	plate	pool	preview
page	peach	phonics	play	post office	pride
pair	peaches	photo	played	praise	puddle
pane	peak	photograph	playful	pray	pulling
park	pear	pick	playing	prayed	puppies
part	peek	pie	please	prefix	purple
partly	pen	pine	pleasing	prepare	purse
patch	pencil	pitch	plow	present	putting
patchwork	people	pizza	point	press	puzzle
path	permitted	plan	poke	prettiest	
Paul	pet	planning	police officer	pretty	

Q

quack	quest	quiet	quilt	quiz
queen	quick	quietly	quit	

R

rabbit	read	rejoice	riding	roll	royal
rain	real	reopen	right	roof	rubbed
rainbow	reason	repent	ring	rope	rubber
ran	recycle	replay	rinse	rough	run
rang	reed	return	road	roughly	rung
rattle	referring	rich	rock	round	running
reaches	refill	riddle	rode	row	

Horizons Spelling Grades 1-3
Cumulative Word List (Cont.)

S

sack	season	shouldn't	sky	someone	stop
saddle	second	shout	sleep	something	stopped
sadly	see	showing	slip	son	store
sadness	seek	sick	slipped	song	storm
said	seen	sickly	slow	soon	story
sail	September	sickness	small	south	stove
same	serve	sight	smaller	spaghetti	straight
sang	seven	sign	smallest	speak	stranger
sat	seventeen	sin	smart	spell	straw
Saturday	seventh	since	smell	spelling	street
sauce	seventy	sing	smile	splash	string
Savior	sew	sinned	smiling	spoon	stripe
saw	shall	sip	smoke	spray	strong
say	she	sir	snack	squeak	stronger
scarf	sheep	sister	snail	squeal	strongest
scarves	shell	sister-in-law	snake	stagecoach	such
scene	shepherd	sit	snow	stand	summer
scent	she's	six	snuggle	stare	sun
school	shine	sixes	so	start	Sunday
science	ship	sixteen	soak	state	sung
scissors	shirt	sixth	soap	stay	supper
scribble	shoe	sixty	sock	stem	surprise
script	shoeless	skate	softer	stick	swallow
scrub	shook	skip	softest	stir	swimming
sea	short	skipping	some	stone	swing
search	should	skirt	somehow	stood	

Horizons Spelling Grades 1-3
Cumulative Word List (Cont.)

T

tackle	thank	thimble	thumb	tool	tries
tagged	thankful	thin	Thursday	tooth	true
tail	thanking	thing	tie	top	trust
take	Thanksgiving	think	tightrope	topped	truthful
tale	that	thinner	tile	torches	trying
talk	the	thinnest	time	toss	tub
tall	their	third	tip	tough	tube
tan	theirs	thirteen	to	tougher	Tuesday
taught	then	thirty	toast	toughest	tug
tax	there	this	today	tower	turkey
tearful	these	those	toe	town	turn
tells	they	though	together	toy	twelve
ten	they'll	three	tomorrow	toys	twenty
tenth	they're	throne	tonight	trail	two
tested	they've	through	too	train	
than	thick	throw	took	tree	

U

uncle	unfair	unlike	unsafe	use
under	unhappy	unload	until	used
undo	United States	unlock	unwrap	useful
uneasy	unjust	unpack	up	using
uneven	unkind	unrepentant	us	Utah

248

Horizons Spelling Grade 3

Horizons Spelling Grades 1-3
Cumulative Word List (Cont.)

V

valentine	verb	verse	very	visit	volleyball
vegetables					

W

wait	watch	weigh	which	winning	work
waited	watches	well	while	winter	world
walk	water	we'll	whisper	wish	worn
wallpaper	wax	went	whistle	wishes	wouldn't
walls	waxes	were	white	with	wound
wanted	way	weren't	who	without	wow
warm	we	we've	whole	wonder	wrap
was	weak	whale	whose	wonderful	write
wash	weapon	what	why	won't	wrong
washes	wear	wheat	will	wood	
washing machine	Wednesday	when	win	wool	
wasn't	wee	where	wing	word	

X-Y-Z

x-ray	yam	yearly	yes	you'd	you've
xylophone	yard	yell	yesterday	your	zero
yak	yawn	yellow	you	you're	